Polishing Treasures

Unveiling Your Worth and Purpose

by

Ylodia Robinson

Copyright © 2015 by Ylodia Robinson
All rights reserved.

No part of this publication may be reproduced, stored in a retrieval system, or transmitted in any form or by any means – electronic, mechanical, digital, photocopy, recording, or any other – except for brief quotations in printed reviews, without the prior permission of the publisher.

Cover Designer: Jessica Richardson
Edited by Autumn Conley

ISBN 9780692629840

Scriptures included in this work are taken from several versions/translations of the Bible, including King James Version (KJV), New International Version (NIV), New American Standard Bible (NASB), and others.

Table of Contents

Dedication..4

Acknowledgments......................................5

Premise...6

Introduction...11

Chapter 1: Being Connected to the Vine.......16

Chapter 2: A Renewing Mind......................30

Chapter 3: Transformation..........................70

Chapter 4: The Joy of Growing..................108

Chapter 5: Pursuing God...........................153

Chapter 6: Faith for the Journey................179

Chapter 7: Living Your Purpose.................188

Chapter 8: Knowing Your Worth................213

About the Author......................................225

Reader's Note..227

Dedication

This book is dedicated to my loving husband. You have been my rock and my source of inspiration. I also dedicate this work to my children, Chloe and Isaiah. Thank you for your intriguing excitement, patience, and support in the birth of this book.

Acknowledgments

With special thanks to the women of God who are in my inner circle. May God continue to bless you with wisdom as you share and impart to others in such loving, committed way. Your encouragement to love the Lord our God with a fierce, powerful, but humble demeanor has opened my eyes and allowed me to see why I need to enter in His presence.

To my heavenly Father, thank you for seeing in me what I struggle to see in myself, an invaluable treasure.

Premise

One evening, I was reading my children's *National Geographic Kids Almanac,* as I skimmed through information about birthstones. I had no particular interest in them, but I continued to read, and before I could stop myself, I had perused the entire article. The importance of what I discovered in those pages is not limited to the facts I learned about the stones; far more significant was the revelation that came to me in the wake of my newfound knowledge. The colorful book displayed pictures of all twelve birthstones in their natural state, as well as photographs of the end products, what the gemstones look like after they are collected and cultivated. The challenge for the reader was to match the natural birthstones to the finished ones. I had limited knowledge about birthstones and how they looked in their raw form, so my approach to that educational activity was basically a process of elimination, based solely on appearance. I looked at the physical features of each raw stone, taking special note of their colors, and then made an educated guess to match to the finished stone. When I completed the exercise, I checked the answer sheet to see how many correct guesses I had made. I was quite surprised to find that my process of elimination worked for some of the stones but did not help me correctly match them all.

As I continued to read more about the stones, I discovered that gemstones in the field hardly ever look like the gems we wear in our jewelry or use as decorations. Rather, they are dull, with rough edges, and they often resemble plain rocks. Before the stones can be called gems, they must be worked on.

A lapidary is an artist or artisan who forms stone, minerals, or gemstones into decorative items such as engraved gems or birthstones. After I read that and learned about gemstones, a greater lesson was revealed to me by God. My eyes were opened to an exciting truth: He is our lapidary, and we are His precious gemstones! My first reaction to this enlightenment was, "Wow, God! You spoke to me through my kids' science book." Even though I may appear dull and unattractive, God is the greatest of craftsmen, and He is polishing me, cutting through those hard places in my life to reveal the beauty beneath. This message was so loud and clear that I wanted to share this revelation with everyone!

Like a stone that has to be worked on before it is called a gem, an unbeliever has to be worked on by God in order to be called a child of God. It was comforting for me to know that under the surface of my hardness was a special gem, waiting to be unveiled. In a profound way, we are Christians in the field of life. Consider the field at different times: your marriage, profession, relationship, parenting, character, finances, and health. All of these areas of our lives sometimes reflect a dull moment, one that causes us to cry out in desperation, and this can cripple our spirit. I want to encourage you that even when an area of your life seems dull and worn, you can trust that God is still polishing and cultivating us to be special gems for His kingdom. I am convicted that when we allow God to mold and shape us, just like the lapidary who cuts, polishes, and designs those stones into precious gems—so can God transform all areas of our lives, as long as we stay connected to Him.

My hope is that every reader of this book will realize how special you are in God's sight and that, in order for Him to polish us; we must valiantly go through the stages of life.

Introduction

Six years ago, I decided to do something that would change my life forever. Prior to this life-altering decision, it was an option I had felt deeply compelled to explore, but I'd never been able to follow through with it. On several occasions, I was convinced that it would be the right thing to do, but my fear always won out in the end. I was afraid of failing, but most of all, I was afraid of doing it by myself. After twenty-plus years of living, life still felt empty, and nothing seemed able to fill that void. In my eyes and the eyes of many around me, I had everything—marriage, child, profession, home, family, and friends—but

I still came up empty. My emptiness was inevitable, because something *was* missing. I was afraid to do that one thing that had been tugging at my heart for years, and I'd ignored it for as far back as I could remember. Sometimes the thoughts were penetrating, but through it all, I was far from what my soul deeply craved. *Is time running out on me?* I wondered. *Should I even care?* Sometimes I was frightened by the reality that my life will not last forever; the thought of dying often overwhelmed me with anxiety. I lived in utter fear that if I died, I would take my last breath lacking that one thing. Many around me seemed to have it, but I was often discouraged, because they did not seem to be happy with it. Thus, for most of my life, I chose to live without it, until one night when I was awakened by it. At that point, I knew, without a doubt, that I had to have it. I remember it like it just happened yesterday, being awakened from a deep sleep, haunted by a dream so intense that I knew it was time. I knew the moment had come for me to grasp what I so desperately needed, that thing that had been calling out to me for so long.

That day formed a distinction in my life; it was my ultimate crossover into a new realm. It was a cold winter morning, about two a.m., when I was awaked by an unusual dream; frantic, with tears running down my cheeks, I woke my husband to tell him I was ready. Looking back, I vividly remember the evidence of sleep in his soft eyes, his confusing facial expression as he tried to accommodate my sudden outburst in the wee hours of the morning. I explained to him that I'd had a dream and that I had to give my life to the Lord. I told him I needed his support, and he nodded in agreement; it was likely easy for him to say yes, as he was still a bit overpowered by sleep. I wondered if my exhausted husband even realized what he'd agreed to. At the time, I wasn't really aware that his support really had nothing to do with my decision, as what I was going through was bigger than him or me or even both of us put together. It was a decision that would forever change my life and, later, his. Only time would reveal the outcome of my life-changing decision.

As faith would have it, I finally declared and accepted Jesus Christ as my personal Lord and Savior. I was baptized in March of 2008, my proclamation of salvation to the world. It was in the brunt of winter, but nothing and no one was going to stop me from making my way to the church, even at five a.m. I was propelled to take that step, and I was determined to delay no longer. It was a phenomenal day in my life, but I soon learned that accepting Jesus Christ as my personal Lord and Savior and being baptized was not enough. I later discovered that staying connected to Jesus would be my only true chance at successfully navigating through this journey of life. It was not an easy lesson to learn, and the path to this discovery has been fraught with poor decisions and tough choices, intermingled with moments of greatness. I finally found it though! Jesus is my Savior! In Him, I am everything, and without Him, I am nothing.

Chapter 1

Being Connected to the Vine

Emptiness

The profound emptiness I experienced in my quest for purpose was not filled by any of the temporary things I had possession of. Although I enjoyed a certain degree of satisfaction and a few accomplishments in life, something was missing. Even with the realization that my life had progressed over a period of time, that constant, underlying joy was missing. I was a good citizen, with responsibilities and obligations, yet ever so often, that ugly, nagging feeling sometimes resurfaced—that feeling that something was missing—especially during the difficult, challenging times in my life. Subsequently, I had to depend on happenings for me to experience joy. In the dull moments, negative thoughts seemed to easily invade my mind and drown out any lingering happiness. I wondered, Could this be triggered by the expectations I have for myself, or am I trying to fulfill the expectations of others? As hard as I tried to fill the various holes in my life, they felt like they continued expanding. I feared that before long, I would fall in, head first.

I needed to remember a familiar scripture: "I am the vine; you are the branches. If you remain in me and I in you, you will bear much fruit; apart from me you can do nothing." (John 15:5 NIV) There was an alarming truth in my quest for purpose, and I knew I was not going to successfully find that purpose until I aligned myself with the vine. Looking back, I have to wonder why it took me so long, why I ran from the very thing I craved. Today, I am transformed by the promised renewing of my mind. I no longer think the way I used to, for my thoughts now fall in line with fulfilling the purpose God has for my life.

Admittedly, I would not have experienced true love if it was not for God's grace. The divine truth is that it was always there, even before I was born: "I knew you before I formed you in your mother's womb..." (Jeremiah 1: 5 NIV) Nevertheless, I continued living in sin day after day, month after month, year after year. I never felt good. I lived in fear, and I was empty. Nevertheless, even when I was lost, God kept me through His amazing grace. What I ran away from for years became the stabilizing source in my life. Consequentially, I am confident in Christ, and I want to share with you the everlasting love God has for us all. The scriptures tell us, "He was in the beginning with God. All things came into being through Him, and apart from

Him, nothing came into being that has come into being. In Him was life, and life was the light of men." (John 1:2-3 NASB)

My thirst was innate. What I really longed for, even though I didn't recognize it at first, was the God in me. Metaphorically speaking, my branches were severed, and, thus, withering. I was made to have a relationship with the Creator of my being, but at that point, this aspect of my life was dead. It was slowly debilitating my marriage, parenthood, profession, and relationships. You might ask how. For some clarity as to why my life was empty, let's consider two scenarios involving a cell phone.

The life of the cell phone is dependent on the charge of the battery. If one removes the battery from the cell phone, it is dead. On the other hand, if the same cell phone battery is not charged but is placed in the cell phone, the likelihood of using the cell phone is nil. In both cases, the phone is dead. Though the body of the phone remains intact, one cannot utilize the phone features without power from the battery. Not only that, but the battery must be connected to the source of power in order for it to be charged and ready for use. Likewise, as believers, we need to be plugged in to the source if we are to utilize our gifts and talents. When we are disconnected, while we may look the same and seemingly live externally, we will remain dead inside. I realized at that point that my standards of living were influenced by the principles of the world rather than by the Word of God. I was not connected to the vine, so I was not able to maximize my innate features to love as a wife, mother, daughter, sister, or friend. As referenced in the scriptures, the Word of God is eternal. He said if I am in Him and He in me, then I will bear fruit. On the contrary, outside of Him, I cannot do anything. Without Christ, I'm as useless as a dead cell phone!

Is this emptiness filled by Christ alone though? Let's put this into perspective. In the eyes of the world, success is measured by what we accumulate in life, be it power, professional accolades, relationships, assets, wealth, children, or countless other measures; the list goes on and on. Are some of these temporary, materialistic things necessary in modern life? Absolutely! There are things we need, and these serve a purpose. They provide and promote the healthy, balanced life intended by God. Should one strive for these things? I believe so. However, there is a divine order by which God expects us to live. Jesus said, "Seek the kingdom of God above all else, and live righteously, and He will give you everything you need." (Matthew 6:33 NLT) In other words, we are to commit our ways to God first, and everything else will fall into place. What does that kind of commitment look like? I cannot say it looks the same for all people, but personally speaking, I know the emptiness I was suffering was as a result of that divine order being seriously out of whack in my life!

My acceptance of Jesus Christ as the vine helped me to understand and further explore my purpose in this life. As I continued on my journey as a practicing believer, I discovered that it was impossible for me to find any real joy without being connected to the source. During those early years, before I accepted Christ, it was natural for me to use the various agents in my life as a replacement of this source. Whether it was my education, my profession, or the pursuit of romance, marriage, children, or relationships, these all offered some sense of gratification, but it did not last, nor did it sink in internally. In no way am I undermining my accomplishments, and I thank God for sustaining me through those moments, but life was still meaningless to a certain extent, and I was not capable of thoroughly enjoying the fruits of my labor. I was fueled to go to college, graduate, and secure a position as an elementary school teacher. I married a wonderful man I am deeply attracted to and love, and we had a daughter and bought a home. Bearing all this in mind, some may ask what I had to complained about; it might have seemed like I'd hit the jackpot in life. I totally understand that thinking, because I was once there too. Perhaps you are nodding in agreement because you can also relate to how lonely your life felt, even though, through natural eyes, it appeared that you had everything. Whichever side of the table we find ourselves on, even significant accomplishments can leave a void that can only be filled by Jesus Christ. It was that profound lack of the source that compromised my true potential to maximize where I was in my life. Being disconnected from Christ crippled my ability to embrace my accomplishments, to face my trials, and to enjoy to the fullest my God-given purpose. Even though I was fueled each day to perform my daily obligations as a wife, mother, employee, daughter, and friend, I still felt an emptiness and had a crippled sense of self. These feelings resurfaced time and time again, especially when I was having a bad day or facing challenges, trials, and temptations.

At the time of the writing of this book, I have been married for over twelve years. I thank God for sustaining my marriage then and now; however, for a period of time, I was resentful in my marriage. This wasn't intentional, but I simply did not know how to overcome it. Our happy days were few and far between. We knew what was right, but neither of us would follow through with it. We stayed together for various reasons, and thank God we did! Looking back, I can truthfully say that the healthy marriage we enjoy today is a direct result of being connected to the source. Do we still have difficulties? Yes! As long as we are both human and alive, that will be inevitable.

Nevertheless, the hope we both have for our marriage today, the determination and God-given will we have to make it work, far exceeds what we had in the past.

Brokenness

Two of the most beautiful moments of my life were when I gave birth to my daughter and son. Our marriage was unstable at the time, and like many couples, we thought having children would strengthen it. It did, to a certain extent, but the void was still there, and taking care of a new infant only added more challenges. We tried to manage as best as we could, but we knew there was room for growth and change. We encountered some distinct challenges, and there were some things we were very passionate about. Those challenges further led us into disagreements. I believe it is important to note that disagreements are absolutely healthy in a marriage; however, our approach to resolving our differences was not always healthy, and that strained our marriage. Nonetheless, after welcoming our children, we both knew they were very special gifts to us.

When I first found out I was pregnant, it was almost like a newfound love. The idea of a tiny being growing inside of me was exhilarating yet humbling. My first pregnancy was very difficult. In the latter part of my first trimester, I was placed on bed rest for the remainder of my pregnancy. The thought of losing my baby weighed heavily on my heart. I knew of God, because I grew up in church, so I prayed to Him with the hopes that He would hear my prayers. During that time, our marriage was under extreme pressure. Because I was on bed rest, my husband had to shoulder the bulk of our financial responsibilities, which included a mortgage, college tuitions, and other bills. So many thoughts and worries penetrated my mind, and it was far too easy for our conversations to melt down into arguments when money was the subject of those discussions.

As I lived basically in isolation for those months of pregnancy, fears that my unborn child might be born prematurely were constant baggage in my mind. I was distressed and depressed, and all I knew to do during that time was to pray. Looking back now, I can see that God's grace was ever present. I successfully gave birth, and I was so thankful that the birthing process was tolerable. All the pain and worry evaporated with the joy of hearing my baby's first cry.

Welcoming our firstborn was an amazing, divine experience. The true joy of a mother's heart when she realizes she has just given birth to another human being cannot quite be expressed. Unfortunately, the excitement of having a newborn does not last forever. Admittedly, even though my daughter was a delight to both of us, reality set in. Before I knew it, I was overcome with trying to juggle all the many responsibilities that come with being a parent. Overtime, I discovered that as beautiful as she was, it was still not enough. I realized that I was going to need more than just survival skills and warm, fuzzy feelings to embrace my newfound life as a wife, mother, and professional. Looking back now, I realize I wasn't doing things by divine order at all times. In general, self was always present, and in my eyes, I was a victim of my own circumstances.

Scripture tells us, "Do not conform any longer to the pattern of this world, but be transformed by the renewing of your mind. Then you will be able to test and approve what God's will is—His good, pleasing, and perfect will."(Romans 12:2 NIV) I later discovered that my actions were a result of how I think and that my train of thoughts will dictate how I respond to life. I needed a renewed mind, and ultimately, as a result my convictions, that would manifest through my actions. Accepting Christ as my personal Lord and Savior was the initial step that was necessary for me to embrace my journey as a born-again believer. Unfortunately, I did not realize that being a Christian is a process; even though I accepted Christ, I didn't realize that there is more to do and to face beyond salvation. I later realized that the ride is not guaranteed to be a smooth, direct, obstruction-free jaunt that will carry us straight to our destination. Rather, there are bumps, steeps, dead ends, and plain old sin to contend with. Today, I am much more mature in my faith than I was six years ago. I hope you will see, as you read farther, that this is not always an easy process. The good news is that because of the renewing of my mind, I am able to test and approve His good, pleasing, perfect will, and so can you!

Chapter 2

A Renewing Mind

Hope

I chose "renewing," in the present tense, because I believe the transformation of the mind in Christ is a daily process, something that continues day by day. I hope to bring you to an understanding of this through the pages of this book. I gave my life to the Lord in March of 2008, six years ago at the time of the writing of this story. My husband gave his life to God three years later. However, it is not as simple as that. It is not just saying words or whispering a prayer. Instead, it is a deeper commitment, one that I will, with the Holy Spirit's guidance, attempt to describe here.

    I dragged my family to church at five a.m. on a cold winter Sunday morning for my baptism, and I did experience a newfound sense of relief and joy, but after that, it was time to go back to my regular life. In my mind, I knew things would not be the same, in regard to my lifestyle. Prior to my acceptance of Jesus as my Lord and Savior, my life was absorbed by worldly deeds. I constantly tried to please my fleshly desires and indulged in the pleasures of this world. This was something I had to learn over a period of time, and at first, I did not realize that the change I needed to experience was only possible through Christ. The change and renewing of my mind was only possible by His grace. It was that amazing grace that snatched me out of the pits of Hell and broke the shackles that bound me. This did not happen all at once; in fact, it continues to happen even now, in my daily living. Each new day, I receive grace to do what is right and to honor God as He transforms me. It is important to emphasize that while we can do nothing to earn grace, we have a responsibility to be available to God and to let Him do His good works in and through us. Today, I know Him personally, but I cannot take credit for where I am. I am simply thankful that God is faithful.

Ironically, the day after I got baptized, my husband and I flew to Mexico for a week. It was a much-deserved trip that was planned long before I even knew I was going to give my life to the Lord. Those who knew me back then knew I enjoyed dancing. Even though we did not go clubbing very regularly, we knew how to make up for those lost days. Dancing was a very engaging activity for me, and I knew how to work my body seductively. Looking back, I realize I was just seeking attention, and I had no problem luring my husband. Being the center of attention on the dance floor of any club, my hips sure did not lie!

Cancun was our destination, and the nightlife there is exotic. Everyone was partying, drinking profusely, and, as Western lingo would put it, going buck wild! There was no restraint in anyone's conduct, and everyone was just after an endless supply of pleasures. Before I knew it, I was engulfed in the rhythm of the night. My feet started moving, and the rest was history; in no time, I was entirely immersed in it. A short while later, I thought, *Wait a minute. Didn't I declare, just a few days ago, that I chose Jesus Christ as my personal Lord and Savior?* Yet there I was, dancing in the nightclub, to the seductive rhythm of Latin music I did not even know the meaning of. I yielded to my temptations, and I did not know how to stop myself. I felt guilty and ashamed of my actions, and I immediately began to question my decision. The very reason I ran from the decision in the first place was because I did not want to mess up, yet there I was, doing exactly that. I wanted to be holy and blameless, and I had failed already. *What did I get myself in? Am I still saved?* I wondered. Those worrisome thoughts penetrated my mind, and I was consumed with guilt and shame. The Bible says, "Therefore, there is now no condemnation for those who are in Christ" (Romans 8:1 NIV) I had not yet learned that, for I was a baby Christian. In my mind I mistakenly assumed the change would be immediate and swift. I later discovered that I was wrong.

One late evening, we walked into a nightclub, where the music was pumping hard. I felt as though my heart was coming through my mouth. The sensory ceiling lights flashed to and fro with bright colors, silk-ribbon dancers were hanging from the ceiling displaying their acrobatic skills, the stage was infused with smoke, and the bar was swinging and alive with loud, boisterous drinkers.

Why am I here? And why do I feel so strange? This is fun, right? I've done this before, so why do I feel so uneasy. My loving husband wanted us to party like old times, and I wanted to be good company for him. It was the week of our anniversary; and we wanted to have fun as we had always known fun to be. Nevertheless, there was a battle raging in my mind. Initially, I questioned and tried to justify my perturbed feelings: *Is dancing in a club with half-naked people where I should really be? Am I allowed to dance with my husband in this type of environment, surrounded by cigar smoke, alcohol, and loose language? Should I allow myself to dance to such derogatory music, even worse because I am not sure what the lyrics are saying in Spanish?* All these questions raced through my mind as I tirelessly tried to make sense of why I was there. It was then that a Christian's worst enemy showed up.

Fear crept into my mind, even though I tried to push the thoughts aside. I was weak, too weak to fight it on my own. The presence of fear can cripple one emotionally, physically, psychologically, and spiritually. Looking back now, I realize I could have totally enjoyed myself with my husband without feeling any guilt or shame. Instead, I was too self-conscious about what I was doing. I was relying on self and all other manmade Christian "rules" I'd heard of since childhood. In my mind's eye, I was responsible for changing my sinful appetite, my cravings for the things of this world. At the time, my perception of Christianity was that it meant being able to consistently obey. There were rules, rules, and more rules.

For the record, let me make it clear that in no way am I encouraging any behavior that is contrary to God's Word or the principles for good Christian living. However, while it is important to surround ourselves with people of the same mind, practices, and moral principles, our change is really solely dependent on God, who sees our heart. I wanted to please God, and I thought my urge to dance to worldly music would stop. I feared that being in such an environment, participating in activities I had always thoroughly enjoyed, would cancel my salvation altogether and change God's love for me. I wanted to do what was right so God would always love me. I did not realize that He loved me already, that I cannot change that, no matter how much I sin. Regardless of my acceptance of that endless, unconditional, agape love, it was always available: "For God so loved the world that He gave his only begotten Son, that whosoever believeth in Him should not perish but have everlasting life." (John 3:16) I believed in Him, so I would not perish. The requirement for everlasting life was simply to believe in God's Son, and I did. I had known that familiar memory verse since I was a child, and I had recited those words over and over again in Sunday school, but I did not realize the context and content of that precious promise.

My early exposure to Christian principles and Christian living was more theoretical than practical. It was more about learning and memorizing scriptures, information, and rules, without necessarily applying or connecting them to real life. I had to go to church, and going to church meant learning memory verses so I would not sin. As you continue to read, you might surmise that much of my deeply rooted learning of discipleship in Christ happened in my latter years, after having lived most of my life deeply entrenched in sin. Those memory verses were only committed to memory, and I did not fully grasp the power of them or the magnitude of the change they can bring about until far later in my life. God loves me so much that He sent His only Son to die for me. It has nothing to do with how good or bad I was or am, nor did it matter if I loved Him or hated Him. His love is available and will never change, because He already accomplished it all. His love is not irreversible, nor will it ever return void. The scripture says, "And may you have the power to understand, as all God's people should, how wide, how long, how high, and how deep His love is." (Ephesians 3:18) His love is unfailing. I qualified to receive it because of my sins, and so do you.

As for what I was experiencing back in the nightclub in Cancun, it was really just my flesh wanting to do what comes naturally for me, wanting to sin. The Holy Spirit that was now abiding in me after my repentance and acceptance of Jesus activated my conscience and began waving a red flag, saying, "Be careful!" Still, there was no condemnation from there. The only condemnation came from my guilt and shame, because I was relying on my own strength to stop myself from indulging. I was unable to control myself from yielding to temptation, so I began to question my weakness and meager knowledge instead of trusting in God and knowing He was in me. Most of my knowledge about Christianity was drowning in legality and a complex, impossible system of manmade rules. My understanding was purely religious and had nothing to do with the truth or the simplicity of God's love. All of this slowly changed when I decided I needed to read my Bible for myself. "All scripture is breathed out by God and profitable for teaching, for reproof, for correction, and for training in righteousness, that the man of God may be competent, equipped for every good work." (2 Timothy 3:16-17)

Today, I do not have the same appetite and cravings for going to wild parties and indulging in X-rated activities. Again, I cannot take credit for where I am spiritually. I am simply thankful. By God's almighty doing, my change was inevitable.

Repentance: Facing the Hidden Truth

After I returned from Mexico, I went back to my normal routine, but this time, things were different. Every weekend, I looked forward to going to church. It was a priority on my to-do list. At the time, my first child was an infant, and I loved to dress my baby and get her ready for church. Sometimes my husband accompanied us to church, and I was so delighted and excited whenever he was with us. I was thirsty for more of Jesus, and everything seemed so different and refreshing. No longer did the Bible feel like a boring history textbook. I was intrigued, relieved, amazed, encouraged, excited, curious, and enlightened. Something was happening to me, and it felt good. I attended Bible classes, took notes during church sermons, and began to study the Word, looking at it from a brand new perspective.

    I was so excited to purchase my Bible. Looking back, I know that had to be God, because a book, a Bible in particular, would have been the last thing on my shopping list at the time. I could not explain the excitement I felt as I sat on the floor of the bookstore and looked through the different versions of study Bibles. For me, it was like trying to purchase the perfect high-end, designer shoes! The vast difference was that such a purchase would be a true life-changer. It was a very fulfilling experience, and I realized that the hole in my life was beginning to shrink. Today, I can admit that it was the best investment I have ever made in my life, one that transformed me daily. After all, "Man shall not live by bread alone but on every word that comes from the mouth of God."(Matthew 4:4 NIV)

I was thirsty. I needed more of God, and once I discovered that He speaks through His Word, I had my a-ha moment: The Bible was my key to hearing God. I began to read it daily and continued to go to church. I participated in Bible studies and attended adult Sunday school classes. The more I read, the more was revealed to me, and that challenged me to change who I was. It was not easy though. *Who is this man?* I thought to myself. For the first time, I felt like I could see, and all the things in me that were not of Him were revealed. I knew change was inevitable, but I did not know how the Lord would accomplish it. He said, "Ask, and it will be given to you; seek, and you will find; knock, and the door will be opened to you." (Matthew 7:7 NIV) It was the beginning of a journey that is not for the swift but for those who will endure to the end.

Earlier, I mentioned that I did not want to make Christ my personal Lord and Savior, because feared messing up after such an important decision. Clearly, I was just beginning to scratch the surface; hence, my perception was wrong. I knew the emptiness was there, and I knew I needed to fill it with Christ, but it seemed difficult and impossible. I did not want to risk compromising my commitment to the Lord. How many times do we intrude on God's territory, trying to tell Him what to do? The very thought sounds taboo, yet we seem to do so over and over, always trying to do things our way and in our own time. Little did I know that my perception of how I will live as a Christian was skewed by my pride and my previous religious beliefs.

In my formative years, I was exposed to religion but not so much Christ. As a child, I was raised in church. Going to church was the only option in my household, especially during the earlier years of my childhood. It's amazing what happens in the mind of a child when he or she is left to internalize what he or she sees. The initial shaping of my understanding of Christianity was influenced by the varied impressions that were demonstrated in my environment. At an early age, I was of the opinion that being a Christian was too difficult, because there was no way on Earth I could ever keep all the rules, laws, and regulations. I also mistakenly thought that the more poor choices I made, the more times I broke the law, the less God would have to do with me. In addition, the Christian people around me, including my relatives, seemed to have dull, boring, unattractive lives. Most of the time, it seemed that God required everyone to walk around with a serious, somber look on their faces, as if joy and laughter were forbidden. There was no expression of self, creativity, and variety, and everyone seemed to fit the same mold, as if they were all speaking from the same script. They were allegedly so holy, yet they were so disconnected. Even though I didn't quite understand their relationship with Jesus, I accepted it and believed it. Much of what I mulled over as I sat through long, humdrum sermons and testimonies that came across as judgmental and condescending at times made me feel hopeless where my salvation was concerned. That exposure to lackluster, lukewarm, restrictive religion was responsible for the perception and opinion I later formed of Christianity, at least to a certain degree. Inevitably, I came to the conclusion that I had little or no interest in further pursuing a relationship with Christ. From the view point of a child, being a follower of Christ seemed rigid, disconnected, and plain old boring. My views were pretty messed up, and when I was old enough to make my own decisions about church attendance, it became more seasonal and was not a priority.

I must emphasize here that I am not claiming that taking children to church is impractical or unhelpful. In fact, it is a good thing for little ones to be in the house of God. The challenge, however, lies with adults. We must practice what we preach and be gracious in our actions. I am very thankful today for those early introductions to the Word. The proverb says, "Train up a child in the way he should go, and when he is old, he will not depart from it." (Proverbs 22:6 KJV) Even though my early impressions were skewed, a seed was planted, and I heard the Word of God from an early age. The nurturing and reaping of that seed was all in the Creator's hands. As the Bible says, "My Word will not return to me empty but will accomplish what I desire and achieve the purpose for which I sent it." (Isaiah 55:11 NLT) This confirmed why I was empty: There was something inside me that needed to give birth, and it was not my accomplishments, marriage, children, family, or friends. It was a battle of the mind, and my spirit was at risk. Even though I tried to run from it, my soul cried out, and Jesus heard me and answered! "For the Word of God is alive and active. Sharper than any double-edged sword, it penetrates even to dividing soul and spirit, joints and marrow; it judges the thoughts and attitudes of the heart." (Hebrew 4:12 NIV) Even though I had my own misconceptions about how Christians should live, God's Word is so eminent that it was able to penetrate the walls of my heart and lead me to the truth. Thankfully, I soon discovered that salvation is the pathway to cultivating a relationship with God and trusting Him to change me internally. I began to understand that walking with God is a journey that involves Him leading me, and I follow Him wherever he goes. I can ask, with all faith that He will answer, "Open my eyes to see the wonderful truths in your instructions." (Psalm 119:18 NLT) Slowly, my mind was being renewed, and God's Word was beginning to take precedence in my life. This journey once again exposed my misconceptions about the thought of doing it on my own. Looking back on my journey as I continued on this path, I acknowledge that I could not have done it without His grace, and I still cannot.

I continued to seek God and read my Bible whenever I had a chance to. I was a wife, a new mother of an eight-month-old, and an elementary school teacher. Each role was demanding, and among it all, I was also a baby Christian. There were so many things I did not know and so many things I wanted to change instantly. I realized later that struggles and trials are really just the training grounds for us to become strong Christians. As I continued to read my Bible, I began to examine myself, and my conscience was awakened. I saw things in me that I thought I'd buried deep within, but my healing was just beginning. I was afraid of what I saw, yet I was comforted, and I was not alone. In essence, I ran from God because I thought I was going to have to walk on my own, but it was not too long before I realized that God was with me: "I will lead the blind by ways they have not known, along unfamiliar paths I will guide them; I will turn the darkness into light before them and make the rough places smooth. These are the things I will do; I will not forsake them." (Isaiah 42:16 NIV) I no longer depended on self for the journey. I now depended on God to lead me.

Wrong Thoughts

In order for me to gain a renewed mind, I had to redirect my thoughts to be in alignment with the Word. It was like a bad habit, very difficult to do. Oftentimes, I made a step forward, only to make two steps backward in my walk. The process of replacing old thoughts with new ones required consistent training. It is a conscious, deliberate choice one must practice daily. Initially, I failed terribly but only to meet my own impossible expectations. After giving my life to Christ and seeking Him, I began to draw closer to Him and asked for help and clarity on how to live. Deep inside my innermost heart, I had issues, and there were things I had not forgiven myself for, even if God already had. I wrestled with the idea of my worthiness to receive His grace, and I often found myself feeling dejected and angry about the areas of my life I was not too proud of, mistakes and bad decisions that had hurt me deeply. I forgot that "He forgave us all our sins."(Colossians 1:13-14) Why was it so hard for me to accept that I am worthy? I later discovered that it was my pride that got in my way, but deeper in the wounds of my heart, there lurked resentment. It was slowly eating away at me, and forgiveness was breached because I could not see past me.

It was no surprise that my extra baggage came along with me when I gave my hand to my husband in marriage. The weight of walking with extra baggage often pulls one down with the burdens of guilt, shame, anger, and resentment. For me, this sometimes materialized in the blame game. It was hard for me to compromise in my marriage, but what was more alarming was that after I gave my life to Christ, I became self-righteous. I will shame the devil and tell no lie: I was not able to see my faults, and I often thought of my husband as my enemy. As a believer and a married woman, that was a recipe for disaster.

Our first big argument once I became a believer was about my conviction regarding tithing. Not long after I started going to church, I began to feel that I should pay my tithes. In all fairness to my husband, he was not convicted, so this was a source of contention and a huge disagreement in our marriage. Initially, I thought he came straight from Hell. *How can he not understand my conviction?* The answer was simple: He was not convicted! My expectations of my husband's reaction to me paying my tithes were unrealistic. I was so caught up in my conviction that I did not hear what my husband said; I did not even try to compromise or understand his concerns, and I was judgmental and impatient. I was working, so I wanted to give 10 percent of my salary, but we are one in marriage. God sees us a single unit, as two individuals joined as one: "Therefore a man shall leave his father and mother and be joined to his wife, and they shall become one flesh." (Genesis 2:24NASB) Perhaps I was doing the right thing, but my motives had to be questioned.

At that time, I was driven by a self-righteous attitude, one that negated the authority of my husband and was, therefore, in direct opposition to scripture: "Wives, submit yourselves to your own husbands, as you do to the Lord. For the husband is the head of the wife as Christ is the head of the Church, His body, of which He is the Savior… Wives should submit to husbands in everything." (Ephesians 5:22-24 NIV) Consequently, I struggled with the acceptance of my role as a wife, yet this was a command directed to Christian households. My flesh was at war! It was difficult to be submissive and respectful. Not only that, but my perception of the words was quite misguided. I thought this "submission" the Bible mentions would limit my ability to make decisions or to be expressive. I had always believed respect was something to be earned; if my husband did not earn my respect, I certainly was not going to give it to him. It was foolish thinking, and I was in no position to give in to his leadership, which Paul later expressed must be in love:

"Husbands, love your wives, just as Christ loved the Church…" Yet, each time I struggled—sometimes even more than I like to admit—God revealed to me that the underlying issue was not so much my apprehension to give in to my husband but rather my lack of trust in Him to come through for my marriage.

In a profound way, reading God's Word opened up my eyes, and I began to see submission differently—not as the world views it but how God intends it to be, knowing that God has our marriage in his hand. No longer did I believe a submissive woman is weak. On the contrary, such a woman is strong and assertive, but most importantly, she loves the Lord. "Charm is deceptive, and beauty is fleeting; but a woman who fears the Lord is to be praised." (Proverbs 31:30 NIV) My realization happened after the fact, and after extended periods of quarreling, deception, resentment, and prayer, my husband and I finally agreed. Paying my tithes was no longer an issue.

Every believer can attest to the fact that whenever God is growing you, there are temptations, struggles, and hardships along the path. These can sometimes knock you out cold. During my seeking, I did not fall short when it came to having my own close encounters with Satan. Truth be told, it is a relevant component of the Christian journey. We will always have battles, but how we combat the ongoing battles is determined by the thoughts we harbor in our minds. The scriptures say, "The temptations in your life are no different from what others experience… He will not allow the temptation to be more than we can stand." (1 Corinthians 10:13 NLT) It was time for wrong thoughts to be eradicated and new thoughts to be restored. It was time to let go and allow God to purge me of all those things that had chained me down. It was spiritual warfare! I had to be aware of Satan's tricks, plots, and deceptions. I had to realize that the devil will use the people around me, those who are dearest to me, as well as my profession, my health, and my finances to inflict pain on me and my family. I had to realize that he looks for any and every area of life in which he can attack and ambush us. Initially, I did not fully grasped how to fight the thoughts, trials, and struggles, so I did the only thing I knew to do. I began to pray.

My prayer life developed over a period of time and later changed my approach on this journey. Sometimes when I prayed, I did not get what I prayed for. It didn't quite make sense, and that was also a huge struggle for me, but having a relationship with God does not mean you will always get exactly what you pray for. Sometimes, it is hard to see God's plans for us in the midst of our difficult times; however, knowing that God's will for our lives is perfect, even when things look imperfect, teaches us to have faith in

God. Sometimes, there are no visible answers to the immense pain and disappointment we feel on the inside when we are going through difficult seasons. We may be stretched beyond our frame, and it can hurt deeply, but we are never harmed. Those profound moments—like my writing of this book and, perhaps, your reading of it—are a confirmation that we are still here! It resonated with me that Jesus told Peter that He would build His Church upon that rock. Figuratively speaking, Jesus was referring to the fundamental role Peter would play in the foundation of the Church. Peter was the rock that God, the master lapidary sculpted, polished and perfected for His glory and today's Christian population.

  Every experience I encountered good or bad, was God's way of renewing my thinking. It did not always seem that way, especially when my emotions were at play in my experiences. I realized that all the wrong thoughts and misconceptions I was dwelling on had to be replaced with new thoughts. Even though paying my tithes was the right thing to do, the fact that I sneaked and paid my tithes to avoid arguments with my husband was, in and of itself, deceitful. God is a God of love and justice, and I was not demonstrating faith in God to speak to my husband's mind. Instead, I tried to rely on my own self and knowledge. In my eyes, *I* had to fix it. Even though I prayed about it, I did not allow God to work through me. God is not a God of misery and confusion. At that stage in my life, our marriage reflected disunity and disharmony, which are not of Christ.

God's Word teaches us to "…demolish arguments and every pretension that sets itself up against the knowledge of God, and we take captive every thought to make it obedient to Christ." (2 Corinthians 10:5) Still, I held on to resentment, unforgiveness, guilt, shame, condemnation, anger, slander, maliciousness, jealousy, complacency, and selfishness. Today, I believe that God is still unveiling in me His true purpose and releasing me of any wrong thoughts that will negatively affect my posture in Him. I know this will take time, but with God, all things are possible.

The Harm in Harboring Wrong Thoughts

When I was a newborn believer, there were many arguments, and for years, I held on to those hurtful moments. That only led to the problem festering. After I gave my life to Christ, it seemed as if I was being tested daily, and I failed miserably, or so I thought. Later, I realized that every time a sensitive issue arose in our quarrels, God was really showing me that I needed to address those areas of my life. Today, I can express that during those moments, I failed to see those trials as life lessons. Rather, I saw my struggles as defeat, but God was hinting to me that I needed to remove that from my life in order for me to grow. For a long time, those wrong thoughts I harbored captivated my mind and took up territory in my life. They were so subtle that before I even realized it, I was setting up myself for failure. I eventually found myself right back where I started.

Paul explained that we do not fight against flesh-and-blood enemies but against evil rulers and authorities of the unseen world, against principalities of darkness and evil spirits in heavenly places. (Ephesians 6:12) Subsequently, we must put on the full armor of God so we can stand firm against the schemes of the devil. (Ephesians 6:11) Harboring wrong thoughts that conflicted with Christ standards compromised my ability to stand firm. I was torn between my worldly way of living and my new commitment to Christ, and that was not enough.

The raging war we fight is in our minds. This is the spiritual warfare we face each day. It may not look like a scene from the *Exorcist* movies, the way Hollywood portrays demon possession; however, Satan fights us strategically and cleverly, using every evil resource at his sinister disposal. He is very powerful, and he unleashes that power on our minds because he is unable to be present everywhere. If we guard our minds with the Word of God and His promises; we can resist the devil, and he will flee.

The Presence of Doubt

Am I truly saved? In every moment of despair, I asked this question and others: *Do I truly understand what it means to be saved? What does it really look like?* I didn't quite understand the validity of my newfound relationship in Christ. I didn't realize that I cannot un-save myself and that my salvation was a gift. Again, I was confused. I thought I had to give something to receive that precious gift, but all was required of me was for me to accept it. Initially, I struggled with the concept of being saved, especially when I messed up and still committed sins. I often doubted my salvation: *If I am really saved, why do I lie? How can I be saved if I still make such bad decision?* However, I continued to seek the Lord. Scripture confirms that if we seek, we will find; that if we ask, it will be given; that if we knock, the doors will be opened. (Luke 11:9)

I was thirsty for more of God, and I knew that outside of Him, I was lost. I hoped He would give me clarity that would conquer my doubts, and He eventually did. God is so faithful that He later brought it to my attention, from studying His Word, that by grace I am saved through my faith. (Ephesians 2:8-9) I encourage you to read more of this passage, but it was my confirmation that I was truly saved. My willingness to read the Bible, attend church, and get involved in the ministry contributed to my growth in Christ. I wanted to know God, wanted to be more like Him. I have to admit that at first, I wanted to do it my way, but that soon changed.

Learning more about God and His love for me drew me closer to Him and Him to me. God wants to change us, to make us more like Him. He is sovereign, but He allows us free will. He could have made us like robots, programmed to do His will all the time, but in His deep love for us, He gifted us with choices. I believe it is our responsibility to make the right ones, but even when we do not, even when we make the worst of decisions, God can turn any situation around. We must only sincerely pour our hearts out to Him in repentance.

One area in my life that God so gently tapped into was learning to accept who I am. I was not confident, and I relied on the validation of others for any sense of self-worth or value. I was not comfortable with how God made me, and for a long time, I dressed up that lack of self- worth and insecurities behind hair weaves, wigs, and anything that helped me escape from revealing even my real, God-given hair.

As a little girl, I had always admired the long, flowing locks of my peers and classmates. I envied their straight or wavy long hair, and I didn't feel that short hair was attractive or beautiful. I did not like my hair because it was short and kinky. I did not feel beautiful because no one told me I was. Not only that, but at times, I was mocked or teased for being shades darker than some of my peers and family members. Little did I realize that my negative perception of who I am was unfortunately derived from family members, who instilled that in me at an early age, diminishing my confidence and self-worth. At a very early age, the mark of the ugly duckling was sealed upon me. As I grew, so did that horrible self-perception, and for many years, I was incapable of loving myself in any regard. I suffered from very low self-esteem. In my eyes, I would never morph into that beautiful swan. To my relatives' credit, I am not sure they knew any better. Regardless, though, it took God's loving grace and mercy to transform my beliefs about myself. He showed me true love and revealed my real worth. I did not like much about my kinky hair, dark-chocolate skin, or my bright, dark brown eyes. I was not pleased by what I saw in the mirror.

    I became obsessed with my hair, constantly trying to think of ways I could change it to better my outward appearance. Exploring different hairstyles, as early on as high school, became a habit that I later regretted. For over twenty years, I refused to be seen in my own hair, the hair God gave me. I spent an exorbitant amount of money on braiding, hair weaves, and wigs. As soon as I took one off, I replaced it with another. My husband loved me either way, but he preferred my natural hair. Sadly, that did not make any difference; I could not see the same beauty in myself that God or my husband saw.

In spite of this, I was very good at displaying false confidence in certain circumstances. Deep inside, though, even when I seemed to fit right in, I was crying out. I struggled internally, and it was killing me slowly. I did not love me. God knows our deepest secrets, and He is very good at revealing them to us so that He can heal us. God got to the root of my problem: I needed to learn to love myself. If I am unable to love me, then I am unable to love my neighbor as myself, which is the second greatest commandment. (Mark 12:31)

As I vividly recall, my parents, siblings, and relatives never told me I am beautiful. This is not part of our culture, but the lack of reinforcement hindered my self-confidence for a long time. At an early age, my hair was chemically processed, but I was so excited when my curly kinks straightened out. *This must be beautiful,* I thought. Even though I still struggled with my dark-chocolate complexion, having my hair processed was redeeming! As that little girl grew up, she constantly tried to beautify herself by continuously enhancing her hair. Unfortunately, my disdain for myself grew along with me, and this was only more difficult in a world that often portrays women as classic sex symbols.

After years of processing, chemical treatments, braids, weaves, and more weaves, my hair line began to recede. By the time I was twenty-six, I had no hair line, and I was forced to make the decision to stop weaving and braiding my hair, for failure to comply would have resulted in early balding. After years of braiding and weaving, I ended up having to make routine visits to a dermatologist for scalp treatments. It was an absolute nightmare! The treatment consisted of injections into my hairline to treat the baldness and, hopefully, stimulate new hair growth. When I looked in my bathroom mirror, I cried. In the midst of it all, I was determined not to let anyone see me without hair, with the exception of my husband, the doctor, and my hairstylist, who one day said, "Girl, why are you wearing a wig?" I answered, "Because I'm not comfortable wearing my hair low. I look like a boy," to which he countered, "You don't need the wig. Your boy cut suits you." Please don't judge me, but after that, the wig became my new best friend, and the deception continued until I became pregnant with my first child. At that point, the denial was over.

Chapter 3

Transformation

Walking in Obedience

It was time to face the real me, hair or no hair. It was time to be comfortable in my own body and skin. Shortly after I became pregnant with my first child, something began to evolve in me. I didn't quite understand what was happening, as you will later discover. I finally had the courage to wear my own hair, kinky and low. It was during that time that I began to notice other women with their hair kinky, short, big, or styled however they chose. There was something special about them, something that made them stand out: Those ladies were confident, and they loved their unique hair! Admittedly, being aware of that did not make it any easier for me to wear my own hair. That took a lot of convincing, and I relied heavily on others' approval or validation before I finally decided to brave it and wear my own hair.

You may wonder why I am sharing this with you and why such a seemingly trivial matter as hairdo would even matter. It is important because it indicates that my internal struggle about myself and my own image was corrupted by what I was exposed to inadvertently by the media, family members, peers, society, cultural norms, and, most significantly, by me. I internalized all that negativity and accepted it as if I was being served gourmet food on a silver platter. I had the choice to refuse to believe or accept what other people thought about me, but I didn't. In my opinion, this is true for thousands of women. My struggle with low self-esteem and lackluster self-confidence was not unique to me. Somewhere right now, out there in our world, there is a little girl or a woman who has experienced or still is experiencing rejection, low self-esteem, and low confidence—not because she wants to but because she doesn't know how to stop it. The world's standards are more superficial than genuine, and if you do not know your value, it becomes very easy to accept the value placed on you by others.

    Why was I unable to block those negative thoughts? To answer that question, I'll share with you what I discovered. It is amazing just how much we can accomplish when we seek answers from God's Word, and the profound wisdom in His Word was the beginning of hope for my transformation. The Bible says we were fearfully and wonderfully made by our Creator and that He made us in His image.(Psalm 139:14, Genesis 1:27) The freedom that comes with this truth was my passport to greater recovery from my own evil devices and society's wrongful and limited definition of beauty and self-worth. Today, I wear my hair as an expression of self, creativity, and my own uniqueness. I no longer try to fit in. Instead, I accept the challenges of being different, fearful, and wonderful. God is concerned about every detail of our lives. Surely you would want to know a God like that personally! He allured me during that fundamental transformation of my life. He was in it, His definition of beauty far outweighed the expectations of the world.

Being Vulnerable

When I gave my life to Christ, I did not quite understand the power of grace until I was able to ignite that fire within me that was waiting to be lit. I was then fueled to learn more about God's righteousness, but the more I sought Him, the more He revealed to me the constant need for change. It did not make any sense to me when I was going through my tests and trials, and in most instances, I played the victim of my own circumstances. Looking back now, I realize that God's hand was working in my life then, just as it is today. He promised, "I will never leave you nor forsake you." (Hebrews13:5 NLT) It took me some time to accept it, but God will not move a situation out of our lives until we have truly dealt with the source of it. How comforting it is to know that He was with me through it all and still is, just as He is with you?

It is amazing how one can appear to have it all together but still harbor a void deep inside. What's worse is that if that void is filled with the wrong things, it can lead to critical self-destruction. My poor self-image crippled a part of my life for such a long time, even though it did not manifest itself in my outward appearance and activities. Internally, I was consuming negativity, a byproduct of resentment. Every day, the news is fraught with stories of people committing suicide. No one is immune, and people of different religions, ethnic groups, or socioeconomic classes too often fall prey to the tragic decision to take their own lives. In my opinion, developing a true relationship with Christ is an effective counteraction to combat life's tendency to carry us to very dark places. A relationship with Christ gives one hope, self-worth, purpose, and direction. Yes, there is a price we must pay, but it is entirely worth it. There is a popular belief that we can do whatever we want in the body of Christ, as well as outside of Christ, but this is, at best, self-deception and, at worst, a bald-faced lie. "For we are God's handiwork, created in Christ Jesus to do good works, which God prepared in advance for us to do." (Ephesians 2:10 NIV) Even though I was saved, I was not fulfilling the good works God had prepared in advance for me to do. My walk was not purpose driven, as I was still disoriented and trying to make sense of my new commitment. Old thoughts had to be replaced with new ones, and it was time for me to be intentional about what occupied my mind. It was time to think on those things that are excellent, honorable, pure, lovely, noble, praiseworthy and admirable. (Philippians 4:8) It was my responsibility to seek God daily, and I had to position myself in alignment with Him for my transformation to begin.

God made us unique because He has unique plans for us. Do you know what your value is in Christ? I must admit that I did not know, but I cannot begin to reiterate enough that God is faithful. Paul was understandably confident that God, who began a good work in us, will perfect it until the day of Christ Jesus. (Philippians 1:6)

I continued to pursue God and His righteousness because I was hungry for more, and I was being fed by His Word. For anyone who has ever tried to eat healthy, you understand that sometimes, you come across flavors that are not necessarily delightful on your palate. Junk food, sweets, and fast food that are very bad for us often taste much better. However, if we continue in unhealthy eating habits, the end result will inevitably be medical complications and body ailments. It is the same if we harbor wrong thoughts. Over a period of time, these accumulate and begin to affect our actions. This is not unique to sinners; believers can and do harbor wrong thoughts. Some of us grow as a result, but many remain in denial, either by disobedience or default.

There was a significant point in my life when I was detached from the people I love. This detachment was a result of the profound resentment boiling inside of me, though at the time, I was not aware that it had corrupted my thoughts and actions. That deep, damaging resentment was detrimental to my spiritual growth and my walk with Christ. I was consumed with grudges, bitterness, anger, and reproach. I was truly living in denial, and I justified my feelings of resentment based on my standards. Subsequently, I thought I had forgiven people I thought had offended me, but, truth be told, part of me did not truly let go of those ill feelings. The act of forgiveness takes time and must be constantly pursued in order to effect change. If unforgiveness resurfaces in some undignified way, it may be a good indication that one has not totally forgiven. For years, I lived with resentment against many of the people I loved dearly.

As I read the Word and asked God to transform me, He revealed to me that I had to deal with this sin. I was a prisoner of my own feelings. Webster defines *resentment* as "a feeling of indignant displeasure or persistent ill will at something regarded as a wrong, insult, or injury." My resentment against others was contaminating my relationships. It affected how I communicated with the people in my life, and it blinded my ability to see the good in every situation. My inability to forgive, bitter hatred, and grudges were a result of my resentment. Within me lurked the side effects of it: jealousy, malice, grumbling, anger, hurt feelings, strife, vengeance, grief, and more. Resentment was poisoning me daily, and where there is resentment there is discontentment. The Bible advises, "Get rid of all bitterness, rage, anger, harsh words, and slander, as well as all types of evil behavior." (Ephesians 4:31 NLT)

    Regardless of what the Word says, I did not really know where to begin. I did not know how to let go of that resentment and bitterness that was holding me hostage. I knew that it was causing division in my household, driving wedges between me and my relatives and friends. I recognized that it was time to let go and let God, but that was no easy task. To be frank, Satan was not having it. The scriptures teach us, "Be angry, and sin not."(Ephesians 4:26 NIV) I didn't even realize that was possible, but as I later found out, "I can do all things through Christ who strengthens me." (Philippians 4:13 NKJV) The good news is, so can you!

Arms Stretched Out

I shared with you the impact of consuming wrong thoughts as a believer and how this can negatively affect your spiritual growth. However, even for wrong thoughts, there comes correction from our heavenly Father. He lovingly corrects and rebukes those things that are not of Him. It was time for me to surrender all areas of my life to Jesus, for His control and transformation. Being saved was not enough. It was time to actually walk in faith, but I would soon learn that the walk would not be an easy one. I have grown to discover that living our lives according to God's will certainly takes a lot of work. At times, it is quite difficult. Nonetheless, I was ready to put my hands to the plow. After God revealed to me that I needed to learn to forgive, I knew I had work to do, but I did not know where to start.

I find it amazing how God orchestrates His power in the lives of His children. From my thirst to wanting to know more about this man called Jesus, I read my Bible daily. I remembered looking at my Bible and feeling overwhelmed. Occasionally, I still have those moments, yet I must admit that constantly seeking Him and His Word has certainly drawn me closer to God through His Son Jesus. I would be remiss if I did not admit that in no way am I where I want to be in Christ; however, I'm certainly not where I used to be, outside the body of Christ, and that makes a huge difference in my journey toward becoming the best believer I can be.

In thinking about this, I am reminded of the story of Joab, when he confronted David after killing Absalom. Though Joab was a wicked commander, he confronted David for mourning Absalom's death. Even though he was a murderer, God used him to speak wisdom to David. This story is one of many the Bible that reiterates that God can use *anyone* He chooses to do His work. God chose me despite my sins, and today, I am a disciple for the kingdom of God. You can be the same if you will repent of your sins and allow Him to grow you. The scriptures teach us that it is sin to know what you ought to do and then not do it (James 4:17) So many people waste so many years trying to "find themselves" or find "the meaning of life," but I have come to a great understanding that the true meaning of life is embedded in our relationship with Christ. Being connected to Christ allows us to be less of ourselves and more like Jesus. The perception that we are here for a purpose is wise, but that purpose can only be realized when we open our minds up to change. During this process, God began to shed me of self, and it was then that I finally realized that in spite of my salvation, I was still an unfinished work.

We are all called to repentance, and repentance leads to the forgiveness of our sins. Repentance gives us a fresh attitude toward God and His righteousness. It is a declaration of our love and commitment, and if we truly repent, we will no longer indulge in our old behavior that is sinful and goes against God's commands.

Following His Lead

Sometimes God physically uproots us and plants us in places we had no desire to go to or ever thought possible. He will do whatever it takes to fulfill His purpose over your life. In September of 2010, my husband's job relocated us to a small, beautiful island in the eastern Caribbean. The idea of living in such a tropical paradise was thrilling and exciting, since I was born and raised on an island. I failed to think about the actual process of making an international move and all the red tape and logistics that would entail. At that particular juncture in our lives, we would be moving with children, and everything had to go. I had moved several times before, but this move involved many moving parts, including two toddlers, coordinating with packers, packing items for storage and shipment, and the overriding emotions of the unexpected. I knew how much the move meant to my hardworking husband and his career, and I really wanted to support him. If I had to do it all over again today, I would still say yes, but my perspective and expectations would be different now. Such is life: Everything we go through ultimately changes the way we respond to life and shapes us to become better people. I love my husband and did not want to be separated from him, so there was no question that I would resign from my own job and fly miles away to be with him and our children, even if it was difficult. However, sometimes even the best of intentions can be corroded by unrealistic expectations, especially when those expectations do not come from God.

As you will later discover, our transition from our beautiful home in the States was quite an ordeal that initially created a wedge in our marriage. During our preparations for the move, we were naturally both under a lot of stress. It was a bittersweet phase of my life, and I harbored some underlying reservations. There were difficult decisions to make, as well as painful goodbyes, and it required us to sever some relationships that truly mattered. Though the distance would not affect all of those relationships, just the idea of being miles away toiled with my emotions. I was afraid, dubious, and anxious, and even the excitement of a Caribbean adventure, of being near those alluring, beautiful, white-sand beaches and in that tropical climate was not enough to stave off my uneasiness.

It all began when I had to resign from my job. Since my childhood, I'd dreamt of becoming a teacher. Lo and behold, that dream eventually became a reality for me. I had settled into my relatively new profession at a wonderful school and was just shy of receiving tenure in the school district, with only a few months to go. I had worked really hard those first couple years and was looking forward to that reward. It meant a lot to me at the time, so I wrestled with the idea that I would have to give up the tenure that was just within reach. Not only that, but I had just managed to relocate my mother to the United States, and we had only spent a few months together. Even though she could visit us on the island, the thought of leaving her in a new environment did not resonate well with me. I felt guilty, but I knew I could not be both places at the same time. My heart belonged with my husband and my children.

I was so flushed and conflicted with overwhelming emotions that I was edgy and bitter all the time, regardless of situations or circumstances. To make matters worse, my wedding band went missing during packing. After hours and days of searching through bags of trash, corners, and crevices, I gave up and prayed silently that it was somewhere in the luggage that had already been packed for shipment. The misplacement of my wedding band weighed heavily on me, but I had little hope that I would never find it. In the end, I never did.

The demands of preparations for our move created space for many arguments, and neither of us found the strength to wave the necessary white flag to put an end to our constant battles. Looking back now, I clearly see that those meaningless, tension-spawned spats robbed us of any joy we might have gleaned from the idea of embarking on a new adventure together. Needless to say, during that significant period in our lives, our true colors were exposed, and my husband and I proved to be our own worst enemies.

When we finally moved to the island, I was overcome with a deep sense of rejection, tension, and loneliness. We had to start all over again, without the support or company of extended family or friends. Initially, as expected, I struggled to adapt to our new environment, and it took a great deal of time for me to get acclimated. I was eventually able to adjust to my new environment, but beneath the smile I tried to fake, there lurked the dark shadow of resentment for my husband. I expected him to react differently, to more fervently acknowledge the sacrifices I had made to support him on that journey, but those expectations were not met. I wanted him to notice and commend me for my commitment and loyalty. I wanted to hear him say, *"Thank you."* I am sure he did thank me in his own unique way, but he did not express gratitude in the way I expected or felt I deserved. I cannot reiterate the danger of resentment in any relationship. Our marriage struggled because, in our moments of outburst and arguments, we both realized that we were victims of our own evil devices. We both resented each other, and it was tearing us apart.

It was not an easy lesson to learn, but on the premise of this huge change in our lives, I can tell you that where God plants you, He will grow you! Even though our marriage was suffering internally, seemingly overrun with resentment and despair, God had his eyes on it, and He was busy making a way out of no way, something He is so good at doing. Though we, as mere humans, wrestle with evil thoughts, God has equipped us with what we need to fight daily within the walls of our minds. We can rest assured that God has not given us a spirit of fear and timidity but of power, love, and self-discipline (2 Timothy 1:7)

Our first year in the new location was tough. I often felt like my marriage was failing, but I did not verbalize it to anyone, for fear of judgment, ridicule, or condemnation. We knew our challenges needed to be resolved in a healthy way, but we could never quite figure out how to make those changes. We were very careful about who was allowed in our marriage, rightfully so, and this is good advice for any relationship. People with wrong influence may cause more harm than good to God's covenant of marriage. We had differing opinions about counseling, so that was not an option for us. We were like waves, tossing back and forth. We both hoped our marriage would work out in the end, but we did not have any plan of action, nor were we equipped with the tools to make that a reality.

In our second year in the Caribbean, my attitude about my marriage and my life changed. I was convicted about it, and I knew my marriage could and would work. God did not want us to have a mediocre marriage; He wanted us to have one that would reflect excellence! Much of this was attributed to my church family at the church I became a part of. Prayer and the Bible-based teaching I received from attending church and participating in the ministry were invaluable. The Bible wisely tells us that we should not forsake "the assembling of ourselves together." (Hebrews 10:25 KJV) Thus, prior to moving, I prayed for God to point me in the direction of a church I could attend for the duration of my time in our new place of residence. I specifically asked for a church home where teaching came from His Word and for a place that would afford me the opportunity to fellowship, serve, and grow in His righteousness. I knew I needed a strong foundation, as I was a new Christian. I was hungry for more of God's Word and teachings. I knew of my imperfections, and I could only make things perfect through Him. The scriptures concurred: "Teach these new disciples to obey all my commands I have given you. And I am with you always, even to the end of the age." (Matthew 28:20 NLT)

I also started a praying wife group, and that prompted me to read several great books on Christian principles that should guide marriage. Initially, I felt a bit inadequate and did not know what I was doing, but to my delight, I later realized that the group provided a healthy channel for women to come together for one cause, the betterment of our marriages. We trusted one another and drew from one another's strength to overcome our temptations, challenges, and victories in our marriages.

God equipped me through those rough periods of my life, and I cannot take that for granted. The impact of seeking God's direction in my life has drawn me closer to Him. In seeking righteousness, I realized I had to die to self. That was the first tool I needed to truly reap the promises of God. It is a remarkable feeling to know that God is with us always, no matter where we are physically and spiritually in the journey of life. God directed our family to Hope Church, which was then called Thankful Family, a nondenominational church. Since I had not grown up in such a church, I was a bit skeptical about it. However, we accepted the invitation to attend, and we have been committed members since. My husband was baptized there, and after years of attending church and faithfully seeking God, our marriage was reconciled. We found new hope in our individual walks with Christ.

Today, we approach marital challenges differently than we would have in the past. I realized that to love my husband unconditionally requires me to see him through the eyes of Christ. I cannot confess enough how much that positively changed the dynamics of our relationship. In one of our praying wives sessions, we discussed our weekly reading from *The Power of a Praying Wife*, by Stormie Omartian. Stormie mentions that when we pray for God in the hopes of changing our husbands, change is bound to happen. Initially, though, that change will occur in us and not in the man we are married to. I was surprised to find that she is absolutely correct! God had to reveal to me—in *His* time and not mine—my own faults, then show me how to grow from them in order to see the changes in my husband.

    I went home from one of our sessions and apologized to my husband for my inability to forgive and let go. In doing so, I felt very vulnerable, but it was also an amazing and humbling experience. It shifted our arguments and disagreements in a different direction. Soon, we recognized that love is not based on feelings, as society likes to define it; rather, it is a choice. That choice sometimes comes with dissatisfaction, hurt, and disappointment. We realized that even though our emotions are valid and indicate meaningful signals that affect our decision-making, loving each other cannot depend independently on our feelings. It must solely be a choice to love one another, even when we are both unlovable. This is the unconditional love that is so eloquently expressed in 1 Corinthians 13. It is the love that God commands for every marriage, and men and women are expected to uphold it. This kind of love is the kind that will last a lifetime, through a plethora of storms. Becoming aware of this truth did not make loving my husband easier, but it challenged me, especially on those hard days, to deny self and love my husband through the eyes of Christ, in an unconditional way. Becoming aware of this truth was fulfilling, but the journey to really discovering the truth came with wounds. The good news is that I no longer internalized my wounds as defeat; instead, I began to see them as a distinct reminder of how strong I am and how able God is. I now know that He can use my wounds and scars to heal me and others.

    Transformation starts in the mind, and faith grows by hearing and applying God's Word. I was not standing on the promises of God when I allowed the enemy to steal the peace and joy from our marriage. Jesus teaches Satan, a thief and the master of deceit, comes only to steal, kill, and destroy. On the contrary, He says of Himself, "I have come that they may have life, and have it to the fullest."(John 10:10 NIV) I was distracted by the happenings going on around me and was not relying on God's faithfulness. In some ways, I was a hearer of the Word and not a doer. I realized that God was trying to get my attention, but I was bombarded by my own selfish ways. There was a battle raging between self and letting go, but thank God my eyes were finally opened, and my mind began to shift. It was time to change, and that change had to begin with me. I discovered that when we rely on ourselves, we will be blinded from seeing the bigger picture of what God has in store for us. If we are consumed by our own fleshly desires and commitments, we are operating from self and not from the perspective of Christ.

Children of God are often faced with trials and temptations, but God looks on our hidden motives. Why do we do what we do, and for what reasons? Hebrews 12:15 warns us about evil intentions. As was the case with Haman in the story of Esther, evil will backfire and consume the one who plots it. Covering bitterness and being superficial is a recipe for disaster in any and all relationships. In the end, we will reap what we sow! Haman wanted to kill Mordecai because he refused to worship him. He cruelly plotted the death of Mordecai and all the Jews, but God had other plans, and what Haman meant for harm to Mordecai, God turned it around for good. The story later reveals that Mordecai sought the help of Esther, another Jew. Being a woman of God and also the king's wife, Esther requested that everyone fast and pray. In the end, Esther was able to save Mordecai and her people. Through it all, they never gave up hope or their faith in God.

    Having faith in God can help us to withstand anything. I didn't immediately see change in my marriage, but I hoped for it and was determine to apply what I had learned to my unique circumstances. Repentance is the foundation of building a strong relationship with Christ, and this will filter into all other relationships.

Acknowledging that we have done wrong and being deliberate about doing what is right is a courageous step, but it is absolutely necessary when we experience change through Jesus.

Too many times, believers profess our faith only in words and not actions. We are responsive to the written Word, but our actions are not entirely reflective of it. God has a way of challenging us to grow. It is during the molding and cutting of our stone (the heart) that God will reveal to us the areas that need to be refined and purified. Have you ever been to that place when your heart is heavy and your mind is consumed with discontentment? If we are being honest with ourselves, we can probably all say that we have. It is interesting to note that this can easily happen to Christians and sinners alike. If we are too complacent and comfortable with our spirituality, that will open a door for Satan to infiltrate and wreak havoc in our lives.

I have experienced and identified many ways in which God can call us higher. First, we must position ourselves to hear Him, trust Him to lead us, and be obedient to follow. Answering a higher calling requires a higher price, and this must not be compromised. Jesus explained this when He said, "If any of you wants to be my follower, you must turn from your selfish ways, take up your cross, and follow me." (Matthew 16:24 NLT) This scripture clearly states what is expected of us. Jesus knew in advance that, as believers, we will be tempted and persecuted for His sake. It is for that same reason that He died on the cross, so that we may have the strength to say no to those things that are not of Him.

One of the most fascinating revelations I have experienced during my journey as a believer is that my sins have been forgiven—all of them—and nothing can change that fact. At first, I didn't quite understand the benefit of this gift. Initially, I tried to surpass all the bad things I had done by keeping score of all the good things. We should not do good simply because we are motivated by the possibility of reward; that is quite different from how God instructs us to live. Taking up the cross and following Jesus is significant, and it involves a daily relationship with Him. In essence, we will never truly understand the extent of that sacrifice, when Jesus died for our sins. He did only good, yet His reward was pain and death. Nevertheless, He was committed to fulfill His purpose, and that was to take away the sins of the world. It is for this very reason that I am propelled, even in my limited understanding, to continue seeking God for as long as I shall live.

I began to thirst for more of His Word. I wanted more and more, and it felt as if I could never get enough! In addition to God's Word itself, I also read all the information in my possession about it. The more I learned, the more I yearned for, and the more I asked. Subsequently, I began to discover the beauty and joy of having a real, daily relationship with Christ. As time progressed, my old habits started to diminish and were replaced with godly attributes and activities. In addition, my views and perspectives began to shift. Realizing the slow but constant change in my life has been empowering, and I am forever thankful. I realized that nothing can separate me from the love of Jesus Christ. (Romans 8:38) It is in that very revelation that I was convicted to know and accept that it is truly an honor to be chosen by God, that I am privileged to serve Him with my life. This newfound knowledge and perspective have influenced my way of life and have helped me to develop a relationship with Christ.

My desire to serve the Lord was motivated by my thankfulness of His love and mercy. I realized that even in my worst moments, God is worthy to be praised and honored. So many times, we easily give up on God, but He will never, ever give up on us. Realizing this truth has cleared the pathway and started the process for me to eradicate resentment, malice, hatred, and anger in my life.

Earlier, I mentioned that being saved was not enough and that experiencing closeness with Jesus takes time, devotion, and commitment. The praying wives group encouraged me to read so many great books: *The Power of a Praying Wife* by Stormie Omartian; *The Five Love Languages* by Dr. Chapman; and a wide variety of Christian principles books, children books, and informational guides. The more I read, the more my knowledge expanded, the more I began to internalize the Word, and the more I prayed for change. I asked God to lead me and to show me His purpose for my life. The more we walk in the purpose of God's plan, the more will be required of us. Serving God with our lives involves work. I discovered later that God expects us to act if we truly believe in Him. We must labor for Christ in love and fellowship, committing our resources and energy. You may ask what that looks like in the life of a believer. It manifests in many ways, because we are all at different levels in our spiritual growth; however, as we mature in Christ, it should be obvious that you are serving out of love. We must be committed with our actions and not just our word, willing to reach out to the widows, the orphans, the backsliders, and the poor; this is being Jesus with skin on.

At this point, you might ask, "How am I supposed to do that?" I understand that this is difficult, for I experienced the same doubts and confusion more times than I would like to admit. The key is to realize that it is not human nature to live this way, and it is not something we can do in and of ourselves. This is where you must let go and let God, where you must surrender everything and place it before God. This is where you must look internally and let your confessions be known unto God. You must say, "My God, my God, here I am! I need you! I am weak, but you are strong!" This is where you level the playing field and cry, "Help me, Jesus!" This is where you rely on His strength and not your own. This is where your prayer life will increase.

Some things in life are a great mystery, such as carrying a human being in your womb for nine months and then going through childbirth to bring a person into the world. Unless you are an OB-GYN, you might not understand the intricacies of how something so beautiful can happen from the semen of a man that is later incubated in the ovaries of a woman, but this mystery cannot be denied or reversed. There are so many things we cannot begin to understand in our natural state of mind, but that does not render it unreal. That is the matchless power of the

God we serve. He is the master lapidary, and He has all the tools He needs to carve and shape us into the special, unique jewels we are. How do you see yourself today? Do you see yourself as Christ sees you? What is your worth? Do you value yourself as being fearfully and wonderfully made? God sees beyond our rugged, displaced, tarnished, dirty, rough shells, for His tools can dig in to the innermost parts, through the thickest and roughest of edges, and shape us into the polished gemstones we really are in His eyes. We can be at peace with the belief that God is in control, and that should be enough to sustain us through our journey with Jesus Christ.

Sometimes we get consumed with the knowledge of Christ and forget about the character of Christ. We get flustered when we misunderstand a scripture or when a sermon doesn't quite resonate with us. Let me use this opportunity to express to you that God is sovereign in all

His ways, and even the wisest man is foolish in comparison to God. Could it be that we are looking too deep, too hard, when God is right here? We will never have all the correct answers to what we seek, but one thing is certain: In God we will find love.

Chapter 4

The Joy of Growing

Salvation

Being saved is the beginning of your relationship with God. As you mature in Christ, you will come to realize that your thoughts and your ways will be His, because He lives in you and you in Him. As a result of reading the Word, praying daily, getting involved in ministry, and serving others, I realized that my concept of the Christian life had changed. Before then, I was self-consumed. I suppose that is normal, to a certain extent. However, the more I started to focus on myself internally, I was blown away by the profound discovery that I am merely a dot in a much bigger picture.

We are all children of God, and He is working together for our good and His purpose. His purpose is for all mankind to be saved, but this can only occur by choice and not force. The very nature of this omnipotent, omnipresent God will not allow Him to force us to love Him, because He loved us enough to give us free will and choice. Realizing how great and loving God is has inspired me to want to know Him more. I yearned to know His ways, His character, and, most of all, to develop a relationship with Him. As you are aware, a relationship takes work and time. It is a mutual agreement between two parties or more. In our earthly relationships, it takes time for us to really get to know our spouses, partners, children, family members, and co-workers. Our level of commitment to these relationships is a good indication of the quality of relationship we desire to develop and maintained. A true relationship with God will include God the Father, His Son Jesus Christ, and the Holy Spirit. He declares, "I am the way, the truth and the life. No one comes to the Father but by me." (John 14:6 NLT) God has extended a personal invitation to us, and it is up to you and me to accept that invitation and show up to meet Him. The quality of any relationship determines the outcome of what is being invested. Oftentimes, we invest in the wrong things and sometimes forget to spend quality time with our heavenly Father. Usually, this is after we decide we have messed up, and it can take months or even years before we realize that we are simply failing to show up to meet God, that we have hung a "Do Not Disturb" sign on the door of our hearts, even when He continued knocking. I was that woman who heard the knocking but chose not to answer, until I was so messed up internally that I had no choice but to cry out. I am grateful to this day that He answered me and that he faithfully kept knocking for all that time.

Are you that person who hears the knock, feels the pull, but just will not answer? Are you being swayed to and fro, not sure what to do or where to go? I encourage you to open the door and let Him in. There is nothing too big or too hard, nothing He is incapable of fixing. Many people, myself included in the beginning, mistakenly think there is some standard route to finding God, a list of prerequisites that have to be fulfilled first; however, that very thought negates the very essence of God. Salvation is not based on principles and knowledge, and it goes far beyond what the human mind can possibly perceive.

A few years ago, I pondered the very essence of God. In doing so, I did some research on the meaning of *essence*. The word originated in 1350 to 1400, Middle English. In philosophy, essence is "the attribute or set of attributes that make an object or substance what it fundamentally is, and which it has by necessity, and without which it loses its identity." Another reference stated that it is "the inward nature, true substance, or constitution of anything, as opposed to what is accidental, phenomenal, illusionary etc." Essence is something that exists in a spiritual or immaterial entity. Hopefully, you agree with me that the above definitions are interchangeable, and common to all three is the recognition that the word means existence, a form of being.

We are all too familiar with the Bible story of creation: Before creation was God, and nothing existed without Him. Contrary to popular beliefs and theological and scientific explanations and references, there is only one truth about our existence, and that can be traced back to the first beings, Adam and Eve. My purpose here is not to be theological, as I admittedly have limited knowledge about the sovereignty of God. However, when we think about the very core of who God is, the three-in-one Father, Son, and Holy Spirit, then we can rest assured that He is present and accessible.

    The very nature of God reflects who He is. I believe that when David felt His presence, it caused him to sing, and this is the reason we are so blessed with the Psalms in our Bibles today: "The heavens proclaim the glory of God. The skies display this craftsmanship. Day after day, they continue to speak; night after night, they make Him known. They speak without a word; their voice is never heard." (Psalm 19:1-3 NLT) It is through the very existence of creation that one can begin to identify and experience the essence of God. The blue skies that stretch across the universe, the depths of the seas clothed in thick clouds, the torrents of water flowing from and depositing into different beds of oceans, valleys, rivers, and lakes, and the waves that roll back and forth from the shores are all too present for one not to notice, and all of these fall under the power of God's sovereignty. The scriptures advise us that our minds are finite; hence, we cannot understand the infiniteness of God in its entirety.

In my opinion, if you find yourself questioning every single word that comes from the scriptures and you become critical and intellectual to the point of no return, you are treading dangerous ground. I believe one can become totally derailed when we try to question every single detail about God and His way. This is why Paul advises us to trust in the Lord. Trust can be difficult, especially when people have failed us. However, let me remind you that we are not dealing with mere man when we think about establishing trust in Christ. The scriptures remind us, "God is not man, so He does not lie. He is not human, so He cannot change His mind." (Numbers 23:19

NLT) Because we do not have all the answers and some things just don't make any sense in our limited psyches, we must trust and emulate those persons who have gone before us and demonstrated trust in God, even when things look funny. The Bible mentions several of these individuals. Trust was required when Abraham acted on what God told him and left his homeland; when Moses' mother placed him in the basket in the banks of the Nile and when he later led the people out of Egypt; and when Rahab hid the spies in her house in the town of Jericho. These individuals exemplify the power of unfailing trust in God's sovereignty. Perhaps you are already aware of how all these amazing stories ended; if not, this may be an opportunity for you to revisit those stories and read them for the first time or again. Note that through a series of strange events, all of these people, among many others, triumphed over their circumstances because they trusted and obeyed. The significance is that these are a reminder and a testimony to us that no matter where you are in your faith, God can meet you right there. As a result, change is inevitable!

He met me when I was lost and unsure, and He has kept me since, even during the numerous times I have drifted or been disobedient. His great love abounds and has not changed. It is that trust and that love that gives me the ability to convey my story, His story to you today.

One Day at a Time

Is there a specific route to seeking Jesus? How do we come to that place of vulnerability? Maybe you think if you stop doing this or that or if you pray more or do not miss a Sunday service, you will find God's favor. If you find yourself in such a place, trying to measure whether or not you are doing enough to really be His, that may be a red flag to indicate that you have not totally surrendered to God. Vulnerability in Christ is where the growth process starts. You must admit to God all your pain, discomfort, hurt, and fear and be available and willing to grow and change. I liken this experience to the rock, as only a lapidary can truly cultivate the stones to ensure that they look splendid. The rocks are at the mercy of the lapidary, but that lapidary takes pride in His work, constantly ensuring that the beauty of each stone is exposed. A place of vulnerability allows us to accept the principles and rules of how God works.

Earlier, I mentioned that I had a very limited understanding of Christianity when I was younger and mistakenly believed it was enveloped in a list of legalistic rules. After all, rules are important, so much so that schools, governing bodies, organizations, and nearly every other facet of society is structured and operated by a set standard of rules. As I continued to mature in Christ, He revealed to me, in many ways, the necessity of rules and why they are for my own good. Christianity is not all about rules, but without any rules at all, we can find ourselves in a world of trouble.

One Monday evening, I had prepared dinner earlier than scheduled. We proceeded with dinner as usual, and the dinner table talks centered on school, work, and daily challenges. After our meal and our discussion, the children were excused from the table. I cleaned up the kitchen, washed the dishes, and decided I would spend some time writing. As I was doing so, my youngest child, who was five years old at the time, asked me if he could do a "water experiment" in the kitchen. I didn't give it much thought, as I was distracted by my writing, so I gave him the go-ahead, on the condition that he allowed his big sister to supervise him, since she was seven at the time, and I assumed she'd make sure he was careful and responsible.

Anyone who has an active imagination and any experience with young children is likely already aware of what greeted me when I entered the kitchen that night. Teeming with disappointment and anger, I started to pick up food particles from the counter and kitchen floor. I wiped water from the countertops and floor and washed another pile of dishes to bring the kitchen back to some semblance of decency. By then, my children were already tucked in bed, listening to a bedtime story being read to them by their dad. I was so furious that steam was practically coming out of my ears, but deep inside, I heard a voice reminding me: *You did not give them any rules, so how could you expect them to obey any?* That voice was right, for I had not instructed my children as to the rules and regulations of water experiments in my kitchen. As a result, I had to pay the penalty and clean the kitchen all over again.

Rules are meant to guide us and keep us safe. Because of rules, we stay on the right side of the street when we are driving. Rules keep us from overdosing on medications and tell us that when we hear emergency sirens, we should immediately pull over to give the ambulance or police cruiser safe passage. Rules are like traffic signals, in that they direct us safely in our journey through life when we obey them properly. On the other hand, if we disobey the rules, there are consequences to face. Oftentimes, our disobedience adversely affects others. Consequently, when we are not respectful of the rules, we hurt ourselves and others. God's rules are no different. When we disobey them, we hurt ourselves, others, and God. Many of the rules that govern our daily functions, administrations, and systems of our countries, nations, and the universe at large are derived from God's Word and the Ten Commandments, whether society wishes to admit this or not. The Bible instructs us not to steal, kill, or bear false witness, and even our modern judicial system sets consequences when we break those rules. Committing any of these can result in incarceration or other penalties in man's justice system as well as God's. Either way, something has to give when we break the rules.

When we break God's rules, which all of us will inevitably do from time to time, He expects us to admit our wrong and ask Him for forgiveness and help to conquer that sin. He will not force us to repent or even to live a sinless life, for He gave us free will to decide how we will live. However, when we refuse to ask Him for help, we will remain disconnected from our almighty Creator, and we will begin to lose our way. This can get very lonely, and before we know it, life will seemingly have no meaning or purpose. As I've mentioned, I have been in that awful place before. I felt such a degree of emptiness for years and was not able to fill it. My life was mundane and insignificant then, but accepting Jesus Christ as my personal Lord and Savior brought me to a place of abundance, though, and I have been serving Him one day at a time since then.

Again, I do not have all the answers you may be looking for, nor do I—or any of us—know how the future will unfold. One thing I am certain of is that God holds that future in His hands, and His plans are perfect, unlike any human plans. The scriptures say, "The foolish plan of God is wiser than the wisest of human plans, and God's weakness is stronger than the greatest of human strength." (1 Corinthians 1:25 NLT) It is this promise, along with many others, that fuels me to seek God daily. This requires time and a hearing heart, a heart that is willing to change. When we seek God, transformation can begin, and we will die to self and the desires of this world. This can be a long process, and it cannot be hastened. It is seldom an easy journey, and truthfully, there is no early destination; this journey continues until death.

As I wrote this, I tried to imagine what my life would have been like without a relationship with Christ, and it frightened me. It would have been pointless, and I would have been like a living dead creature. The Word admonishes us that outside of Christ, we are dead spiritually, even if we are alive physically. Are you walking around dead in the spirit? Are you sick and tired of being sick and tired? Have you noticed that your happiness is short lived and quickly overcome by your circumstances? Well, I have good news for you! It doesn't have to be that way, for there is hope in King Jesus! You can accept Jesus as your personal Lord and Savior and be transformed by the renewing of your mind when you place your faith in Him. The hope that is available in Jesus can change your current circumstances, but first, you must ask yourself how much you value your own soul. If you truly examine your heart and your response is yes, then realize that your soul is important to Jesus.

How do you make the change though? Simple! You must only submit to God, confess your sins to Him, and tell Him that you need Him. This will not take much of your time, but it will be an intimate moment of truth and vulnerability. After that, you will be led, for Christ will live within you. He has promised that He will never leave us or forsake us. If not for the Lord in my life, I would be living an incomplete life. Without Him, I am hopeless, for He came to set the captives free, to heal the wounded, and to help the blind to see. I was once blinded by my desires, living a dangerous life outside of Christ. I was looking for salvation in the wrong places, seeking it from the wrong things. Thankfully, God caught me in the midst of my confusion and pain. I was caught, and if He did it for me, as deluded as I was, He can definitely do it for you!

There is great joy in knowing Christ and having a relationship with him. My views on how to live my life have changed and are still changing as God continues to grow me. When I stop to pay attention to the simpler things in life, I see God in everything. He is in the birds that fly in the air and the raindrops that water the fields of the Earth. He is in the sun that shines so brightly and separates us from the darkness at night. He is in the millions of stars that adorn the black velvet of the night sky. He can be heard in the laughter of our children and in the wind that blows by. He is as present as in the air we breathe. He alone is God, and He is deserving of our praise and lifetime commitment.

Living a life that is totally committed to Christ should not be taken lightly, for it is easier said than done. As humans, we will always suffer from the struggle between the flesh and the spirit, but the unwavering truth is that it can be done, and others have done it. I am living proof of that, my friend! The Bible is a good starting place, the place of refreshment and reference we can run to for encouragement, when we feel as though the journey is impossible. Joseph was sold into slavery by his own brothers, who were jealous of his father's love for him. He suffered greatly from family betrayal, not to mention a deep sense of abandonment. Nevertheless, he was faithful to God, and God turned his situation around. Joseph was raised up from the pits of slavery and placed in a high position that would later benefit the same brothers who betrayed him. God saved Daniel in the lion's den, and he protected David when his life was put up for ransom. These are all familiar Sunday school stories, but there are also significant examples of characters outside the Bible, people who believed and served God.

Dr. Martin Luther King was an active participant in the Civil Rights Movement and a man who put his trust in God. Missionaries all over the world must have faith when they take the Word and offer their time and service in the deepest, darkest corners of the world, in places drenched in war, poverty, and social and political injustice. Apostles, prophets, preachers, and teachers throughout history have made the decision to follow Jesus. Just like them, we can invite Christ into our lives and allow Him to change us.

There must be a desire from within the walls of our hearts, because while men look on the outward appearance, God examines the heart. (1 Samuel 16:7) Is your heart pure, or is it clogged with hatred, envy, grudges, maliciousness, wickedness, doubt, fear, lawlessness, anger, deceit, pride, jealousy, or slander? All these vile things would call for a massive heart surgery! Basic knowledge teaches us that the heart is a muscular organ that pumps blood through the blood vessels of the circulatory system. The heart is such a vital organ, the wellspring of life, yet it is only the size of a fist. The Bible warns, "Above all else, guard your heart, for everything you do flows from it." (Proverbs 4:23 NIV) What is flowing from your heart? From a medical point of view, a heart that is unable to perform its daily function will inevitably result in cardiovascular disease, medical complications, and potentially death, depending on what medical interventions can be taken. The same situation can be used as an analogy for our hearts in a spiritual sense: A spiritual heart that is occupied by sin will inevitably lead to death, as the wages of sin is death. The only successful intervention will be submission of that heart to God, and failure to do so means one will forfeit his or her chance to live forever. The bible tells us that God examines our hearts. One that reflects Christ is a heart that is healthy and in good condition. We are all faced with this very simple but true question: Are our hearts pure?

Operation Grace

We can and should work diligently to pursue heart purity, but God knows we require the gift of grace to carry us through each day. He knows we face a constant struggle between our fleshly desires and the desires of the spirit. Grace is efficacious, in that it propels you to take flight. Grace navigates our every move and gives us hope. Acts 15:11 speaks about the undeserved grace that God has given; in fact, many ministers have referred to G.R.A.C.E. as an acronym meaning, "God's riches at Christ's expense," and this is quite accurate. We inherited God's favor and did not have to work for it; there is nothing we could do, as the sinners we are, to earn it anyway. It is the power of God's grace that saves us from sin, and as a result, we inherit eternal life.

As I continue to seek God on my personal journey, I realize that the more my eyes are focused on Christ, the more His mercies unfold before me daily. I am his child, and He fathers me with compassion. The beauty in the believer's journey is that you can experience constant growth when you stay connected to the vine. It is an amazing experience and is unique to each individual. Collectively, we have the same goal: to one day be reunited with our heavenly Father; however, the way we live while we are here on Earth varies, even if our circumstances are similar. I have grown since I gave my life to the Lord, and I still have room to grow. I have discovered that each lesson is unique and has its own merit. One of my most common prayer requests is that I will not miss any lesson or get distracted by situations around me. Every day is a new day, with new mercies and new opportunities to do good. By the grace of God, we are given each dawn as a chance to try again. We have another opportunity to be a loving wife or husband, a nurturing parent, a reliable employee, or a kind friend. There are endless possibilities and endless opportunities. We can target in on what we can do to make a difference as a believer. The psalmist spoke about the joy of those who seek the Lord and do His will (Psalm 5:11). It brings me such deep contentment and joy when I use the opportunity God has given me to share His Word.

Not too long ago, I received a revelation in my prayer time with the Lord. To some who give their lives to Christ, their purpose seems obvious and clear, but others—like me—have questions. I suppose I was naïve, and I have already admitted that I was a bit tied up with self and that I have my own limitations. Thank God for His patience and unconditional love, though, for He heard my prayer when I asked Him to reveal my purpose. I asked, "Why am I here, Lord? Now that I gave my life to you, what shall I do with it?" I would be remiss if I did not mention that part of my purpose is to tend to my roles as a wife and mother, executing my daily routines and meeting my daily obligations and responsibilities in that regard. However, I wanted to know what God wanted me to do with my salvation beyond the daily duties that befall us all. Before long, it became clear to me that God wants me to share His Word with the world.

This astounding revelation came to me twice in (Jeremiah 1:5 NIV): "I knew you before I formed you in your mother's womb. Before you were born, I set you apart and appointed you as my prophet to the nations." For the first time, my attention was brought to this scripture one morning during my devotions. I had just finished prayer and had asked God to reveal to me His plans for me as a believer. After I prayed, I opened my Bible to look for His answer, and my Bible opened to that particular Old

Testament book. When I read the first chapter, I wondered, *Is this really for me? This can't be. What are you trying to say, Lord? I am not a mature Christian, not well versed in my Bible yet. I am not experienced.* By the time I was finished questioning, I had managed to plant a seed of doubt and discouragement deep in my mind. How many times have you replaced God's words with your own thoughts or the words other people say? How many times do we believe everything else that comes to our attention but question what God says to us in His Word? I am so grateful that in these times, we see the extent of God's grace in our lives, and we can only stand in awe of how great God is to us.

My second encounter of God responding to my question came when I spoke to a friend who was very mature in her faith. I had called her about an experience I'd had and wanted her perspective on the matter. During our conversation, she told me she had been pondering scripture and thought Jeremiah 1:5 might be helpful. Nearly every Christian can attest to the fact that God certainly has a sense of humor, and it was very evident in this instance. I broke into tears with the phone still on my ear as I listened to her quote the scripture I'd recently read. God speaks directly to us, and when we do not hear Him, He sometimes uses others.

God has a plan for me, and He has a plan for you, but His supposed plan for me frightened me. *A prophet?* I thought to myself. I immediately began to focus on my weaknesses, and I had to be reminded that in my weakness, He will make me strong. (2 Corinthians 12:10) I did not immediately accept that honorable task from him, as I did not quite understand the extent of my purpose. I had no idea how it would unfold, but day by day, baby step by baby step, God began to reveal to me how He wanted me to live His purpose. My desire is to be obedient to God's will. Sometimes I do not feel comfortable doing so, but I know the end result of obedience is far more rewarding and is worth a little of my temporary discomfort.

I started to look for opportunities to share God's Word with everyone. I did not need a platform or a pulpit. I only needed that thirsting passion, and sharing became natural in time and flowed freely from the Holy Spirit within me. I knew it was crucially important to share God's Word with my children. The Bible says, "Teach them to your children. Talk about them when you are at home and when you are on the road, when you are going to bed and when you are getting up." (Deuteronomy 11:19 NLT) It was important to share with people in my workplace, my church, and the community. I had to take God's Word with me wherever I went, for the purpose He so clearly revealed to me was to share God's Word and His everlasting love.

There is no greater love than God's, and it was for that reason that He sacrificed his Son Jesus to save the world from the fatal wages of sin. Even though we lead individual lives and have our own unique obligations, far more important than our everyday life is how we share God's Word, His love, and His grace with everyone we come into contact with. As Christians, we are called to be the light of the world, and this requires witnessing to others in ways that will minister to the lost. Jesus saw the need of a dying world, and prior to his ascension to Heaven after His crucifixion, he commissioned them to teach the gospel for all to hear. He commanded them to carry the good news to all. I believe this is the ultimate purpose of every believer, to share the gospel with the world who so desperately needs it.

Jesus said, "The harvest is great, but the workers are few. So pray to the Lord, who is in charge of the harvest;

ask Him to send more workers into His fields."(Luke 10:2 NLT) Jesus knew that many people, myself included, would come to a place of emptiness and would be looking for a way to fill that painful void. He knew that if workers were in the field and harvesting, it would make a world of a difference. If you are a believer, have you been bold enough to share the Word? We are called to be Jesus with skin on. In no way should we be abrasive, nor should we compromise God's Word. Instead, we should gently correct, rebuke, and pursue the lost and lead them back home to their loving Father.

This requires work on our part. We cannot make an impact in the world if we are not confident in what we claim to believe. We can increase our confidence in Christ by knowing what He says, and knowing what He says requires that we meditate often on His Word, read our Bibles, and seek God through prayer and fasting. We must listen and seek His guidance. We cannot win the hearts of men if we ourselves are dubious about what we believe. We must rise above religion and conflicts over denominations and develop a relationship with Christ. We must break through all stifling and dividing legalistic rules, denominational ties, and religious practices. We must get to know God on a personal level and allow Him to be part of our daily lives.

There is freedom in Christ, and He will help you face the impossible and live life to the fullest. I have gained great confidence in God, and this makes a positive difference in the way I approach my life, decisions, and commitments. This newfound confidence has given me the courage to share God in my environment, regardless of where I am. It is living daily from the God within me. Finding God has not made me immune to the challenges of living in this world; however, I have great hope and believe that God is in control of my life. This profound truth shifts the way I deal with my roadblocks. I still have to work on my marriage, I often have to learn new ways of becoming a more effective loving mom, I continue to seek ways of improving myself on the job, I still have to find peaceful ways to resolve family conflicts, and the list goes on and on. Nevertheless, despite the challenges of living, I do not allow my circumstances to define who I am. No longer am I held captive by playing the victim, for I can be a victor in Christ. I know who I am, and when you know who you are, you know what to do. Do you know who you are? Have you found your purpose?

Grace and Mercy

Living a purposeful life gives us a new reason for living. It draws us closer to God and helps us make an impact wherever we go. The size of the impact really does not matter; what really matters is that when we understand the love Jesus has for us, it frees us to make a difference. We are called to be the salt of the Earth. (Matthew 5:13) Collectively, as Christians, we are the salt of the world, an ingredient that adds flavor. This separates us from the rest of the world, for we are change agents, and our purpose is to effect change in a positive way. You may be looking back at all the wrong things you have done, and perhaps you feel unworthy because of those sins and mistakes. The good thing about being a change agent is that if you are not currently fulfilling that role, you can ask God to forgive you. You can repent of your sins and receive His love. Simple, isn't it? Sometimes simplicity helps us find humble beginnings that will later lead to great endings, like being able to live a life that reflects Christ.

    I once felt the need to be associated with a specific denomination. During my earlier encounters with church, I was caught up in religion and not relationship. Since then, I have come to realize that for me to maximize my relationship with Christ, I had to let go off certain notions and beliefs that were common among the people I was raised around. My focus shifted away from those external influences, and I was thirsty for more of God's Word. The more I read and studied my Bible, the more revelations I had. It is easy to read the Bible and memorize scriptures verse by verse, for this is an act of the mind. Far more difficult is applying God's Word to your daily life, putting it into practical action within and around you, for this is an action of the heart. Our sinful nature resists this change, and it becomes a struggle to fight against our very flesh. If we don't deny our natural inclinations, however, it will lead us to destruction.

    Today, I am here to encourage you and remind you of the hope I have in God, through His Son Jesus. You do not have to get it right on your own. You can rely on God for His tender grace and mercy. Every day, He affords us new mercies. When we gasp for that fresh breath of air, we know we are still here. It does not matter how dark our past has been; what matters is that when we seek God, He will help us and show us the way to glory. There are no hidden formulas or escape routes. The truth is in Christ. We have eternal life in Him, but outside of Him, we face eternal death.

There is a dark path of my past that today motivates me to glorify the God of Abraham because I can now see His goodness in my life. When I was about twelve years old, I was convinced that my life was not worth living. Back in those days, children were to be seen and not heard, so I had no channel to express how I felt; if I ever tried to break the rules and speak up, there were always repercussions for my insolence. Numerous times, I was scolded when I did not even feel the punishment was warranted. Consequently, in my plight to express myself and plead for mercy, I often ended up in deeper water and suffered the consequences of lashes or ridicule. On one particular day, I had just about had enough, so much so that I was ready to take my life to put a stop to it.

In my selfish, immature thinking at the time, I felt as if my life was purposeless and that there was no reason for me to continue living. I remember it now, as vividly as if it happened yesterday. I went in the bathroom, opened our medicine cabinet, and popped open one of the pill bottles. I emptied the contents in my hand and swallowed every capsule, without so much as a second thought. No one knew what I was doing, so I just locked myself in the bathroom and waited patiently to die. I lay still for a few minutes and closed my eyes. The silence was loud somehow, and I could hear the rapid beat of my young, broken heart. I was afraid to die, but it felt like the only way to escape growing up in an environment where I felt unwanted and unloved. *Why won't I die?* I thought to myself impatiently. *Why is it taking so long?* I wanted it to end quickly, so no one would find me and try to stop me. Worst of all, I knew I would be in deep trouble if any of my relatives discovered my plot to terminate my own life.

    I waited and waited, and nothing happened, but I was determined. I made my way to the unfinished kitchen in the back of the house. There was some shelter from the roof, but the ceiling was only comprised of plywood to provide some sort of foundation. I decided that I could try to hang myself and that I likely wouldn't feel a thing if I jumped really hard. I was driven then by a force that was not flesh and blood. Rather, it was those principalities of darkness and evil rulers and authorities of the unseen world, the evil spirits Paul spoke of in Ephesians 6:10, but at the time, I was compelled to do it anyway. Without hesitating, I tied a rope carefully around my neck. I knew that what I was doing was dangerous, and I was still scared to die, but I could not stop myself. The pain was too deep, and I was too far gone. I moved a chair into position and stood on it, then reached for the plywood ceiling. Aimlessly, I tied the rope around the wood. When the time came for me to jump, I was very tense, but I closed my eyes and stepped off the chair, not sure how it would all end. It happened so fast and jerked me so hard, but I knew I was still alive when I felt my body hit the hard tile floor.

The rope snapped, but I was not to be deterred in my quest to end my pain. I went into the kitchen and found the biggest, sharpest knife I could and pressed the blade hard against my wrist. Then, overcome with uncertainty, I stopped and began to cry. *Why is it so hard to die?* I thought, but then I mustered up the courage to continue pressing the knife. I could not get past the pain of the knife piercing my skin, so I eventually gave up, put the knife down, and kept to myself for the remainder of the night.

Today, I am so thankful that God protected me, even from the abuse and hurt I was trying to do to myself. He watched over me even when I didn't ask Him to. At that time, I thought my death would punish my family for hurting me the way they had; it was my way of paying them back. Today, I realize I was a lost preteen going through some severe growing pains, but with no direct channel to communicate all my questions, insecurities, and fears I rebelled. I was often reprimanded for things I didn't quite understand, but I did not go about solving it the right way. Nevertheless, God protected me by his boundless grace, even from my own foolish thinking, and it is only because of that that I am here to write this today.

How many times have you experienced God's grace in your life? It is a daily experience for me, something I see even in the simplest of things. I didn't quite understand the magnitude of God's grace until I sought God and experienced a relationship with Him. It is difficult to gain a true understanding of such matchless grace, for it supersedes my natural ability to reason and understand. Still, I recognize God's grace in my everyday life, and I know how much I mean to Him. The Lord delights in the details of my life. Though I stumble, I will never fall, for the Lord holds me in His good hand. (Psalm 37:24 NIV) God had a purpose for my life, and even though I was not able to identify that purpose for a long time, He knew the plans He had in store for me, and dying at age twelve was certainly not part of it.

I am also thankful for the blood of Jesus, for without His precious blood, none of us would have that desperately needed second chance. Many people would have been hurt because of my sin. Sin has the power to blind us and take away our conscious thinking. Not only does it affect the sinner, but it also hurts others. We experience this daily in numerous tragic stories committed by people in different walks of life. Picture a drunken driver recklessly cruising through the streets. His vision is obstructed, and while he coasts way beyond the speed limit, he fails to notice or care about the red traffic light and collides into another car. Just imagine how such a horrible scenario might end. Both drivers, the innocent and the guilty, have connections and acquaintances in life: a husband or wife, father or mother, brother or sister, son or daughter, uncle or aunt, or any number of other relationships. Everyone connected to both persons would be affected by the terrible news, and life will never be the same for any of them. Sin is a poison that affects the sinner and others alike, and the damage it causes is sometimes severe.

Perhaps a husband or wife engages in an extramarital affair. The end result when that affair comes to light, which they almost always do, is that the guilty will have to struggle to save his or her marriage, but it does not end there. The children will be caught in the middle, scared, hurt, and forced to choose between their parents. The little ones who had nothing to do with that sin will be hurt by it.

"For the wages of sin is death." (Romans 6:23 NLT) Sin is controlling, "crouching at the door, eager to control you. But you must subdue it and be its master." (Genesis 4:7 NLT) The Lord had such a conversation with Cain before he jealously killed his brother Abel. Had Cain listened to God, he would have subdued his feelings, but he did not, and much damage was done not only in the life of Cain, but also in the lives of his family and all of mankind thereafter.

This brings me back to my suicide attempt. I allowed sin to overpower me because I did not recognize the power I have to subdue sin and be its master. Like so many are, I was a slave to sin. I was held captive by it because I did not see myself as God saw me. Thank God for grace, for He shielded me, and I was protected. To this day, I have no idea why the pills did not adversely affect me, as I don't even recall being sick after swallowing so many of them. I only know that I lived through the pills, the rope, and the knife, and I am here today, living my God-given purpose because He protected me.

Perhaps you are being held captive by sin, but I want you to know that there is salvation for you too. It requires your time and sacrifice, but you should seek God today, right now, while you can. Death is inevitable, but to die in Christ is a choice that you must make before it's too late. Maybe you have made that choice but you have not given Him your all. You are like the waves tossing to and fro and are not fulfilling your God-given purpose. Maybe you think you are beyond being saved and reached by God. Whatever it is that is stopping you from reaching out to take this free gift of salvation, I am here to bring you good news! Jesus loves you! He made you in His own image and likeness, and He gave you free will; this is a gift, but if you use it selfishly, it can destroy something so beautiful.

It does not matter where you are in your search for answers. Know that God's desire is for every person to be saved. His love is available for all, independent of our acceptance. Christ died once for us, for all sinners, so we might be saved. If you have not accepted Christ as your personal Lord and Savior, do it today! There is no special ritual, elaborate declaration, or perfectly worded prayer you must memorize and recite. You must only open your heart and ask God to forgive you of your sins and invite Him to come into your heart to stay for eternity. If you have done so, congratulations, for that is the first step! Next on your agenda should be to find a good, Bible-based church and become a member so you can begin your own journey to finding true joy and eternal peace through Jesus Christ.

Chapter 5

Pursuing God

His Righteousness

Like I mentioned earlier, giving your life to God is the beginning of grasping salvation. Beyond accepting Christ, however, we must also get to know him personally. Inevitably, this will lead us to sanctification. Your relationship with Christ will be like any other relationship you invest in and truly want to nurture. You will be interested in learning more about Him, and in the process, you will learn much more about yourself in relation to Him.

The Christian journey entails daily growth, for one cannot remain the same in such a relationship. However, growth can be blighted if we do not seek the things of God and allow Him to grow us. This growth, however, is not solely dependent on us. "For God made Christ, who never sinned, to be the offering for our sin, so that we could be made right with God through Christ."(1 Corinthians 5:21NLT) It is important to note that if it was not for Christ, the process of seeking God's righteousness would not be possible. Because Christ paved the way for all people when He died on the cross, God exchanged our sins for His righteousness. Jesus was blameless, yet He bore Calvary's cruel cross for all our sins. Why is this important to know when seeking God's righteousness? Because you simply cannot find God's righteousness without accepting Christ. Only in Christ can you face God. If we are not righteous in Christ, God cannot look upon our wickedness.

If we are not living by God's pattern, then we are living in sin.

Seeking God's righteousness involves your whole being. It involves your way of life, your outlook on life, and the way you respond to life. It involves how others see us and the quality of the lives we live. It involves our commitment to honor God through Jesus Christ.

The book of Proverbs teaches us about righteousness and wickedness in the way we live. There is a distinct difference, and one cannot be mistaken for the other. Whether we choose to live righteously or wickedly, either path will affect all areas of our lives. You may say, "I cannot live righteously in a world that is wicked, where there is injustice screaming through the streets, cities, and nations." You may feel a sense of burden and believe living righteously is impossible, but remember that all things are possible with God (Mark 10:27), and in Him we live and breathe. If we rely on ourselves, we will inevitably fail. On the contrary, if we rely on Jesus, our perspective changes, and we will no longer measure what we see by our capabilities and our own strength. We can learn to look to Jesus our teacher, leader and friend.

Personally speaking, I often confused righteousness with doing what I thought was right. My intentions may have been good, and I tried to do as many good deeds as possible. However, I have learned that even though what I do may be good in general, it may not be good for my ultimate purpose. I have also grown to understand that something done well is not always good. The psalmist talks about the characteristics of his enemies in (Psalm 52:2 NLT): "You're an expert of telling lies." Though that enemy was very good at telling lies, that did not mean that telling lies was a very good thing to do. Likewise, we must remember that not everything we think is good or everything that is done well are the right things we should be doing. We must instead seek righteousness through God.

Seeking God's righteousness requires us to get to know Him through reading His Word, meditating upon His Word, reflecting on His Word, memorizing His Word, and putting His Word into action. Seeking God's righteousness calls us to a higher level, and we will no longer live by worldly standards nor our own. Instead, we live only by God's standards. This is not easy, and God is keenly aware of our struggle, but He expects us to overcome. After all, He sent Jesus Christ to pave the way! Do you trust Him enough to believe you can finish this Christian race? "Everything He does reveals His glory and majesty. His righteousness never fails." (Psalm 111:3 NLT) The prophet Jeremiah also confirmed, "The Lord is our righteousness" (Jeremiah 23:6 NLT) Our righteousness comes from Him, so when we do something right, we cannot take credit for it. We must be humbly aware and conscientious of the fact that our only righteousness can be found in Christ Jesus, for we are made pure by His blood. We demonstrate His righteousness when we do the opposite of what our flesh tells us to do. To accomplish this, we must listen to God's voice and do the very thing that does not come natural for us. We can do this in the name of Jesus. It requires listening to the Holy Spirit's guidance and saying, with a clean heart, "Lord, let your will be done."

In the early stages of my relationship with Christ, I did not understand that it was His righteousness that would make me pure. Oftentimes, I committed the same sins over and over but always promised myself it would not happen again. If you have been down this shameful path, you can relate to that experience. I was trying to depend on my own strength, and every time I messed up, I withdrew from seeking God because I felt ashamed and questioned my salvation. As time progressed, my understanding began to develop, and I learned even more as I deepened my study of the scriptures. Seeking God's righteousness is a steady process that daily reveals to you your darkness and His light.

The scriptures tell us we were all born in sin and shaped in iniquity. (Psalms 51: 5) There is nothing in us that naturally wants to do good. If not for the shedding of Jesus' blood, we would have no opportunity for righteousness at all. In my thirst for more of this Jesus, I read my Bible as often as I could, so I would know Him more. As a result, I gradually began to know myself. Little by little, day by day, my darkness was stripped away and replaced with light. I only recognized this by studying the Word, but over a period of time after being a young Christian, I started to grow. Seeking God's righteousness involves daily growth. One cannot be the same when we study the Word of God and apply it to daily living. Paul expressed this to the Jewish believers when they grew stagnant in their relationship with Christ: "You have been believers so long now that you ought to be teaching others. Instead, you need someone to teach you again the basic things about God's Word. You are like babies who need milk and cannot eat solid food." (Hebrews 5:12 NLT)

Oftentimes, we hear or read God's Word but do not take the time to study and meditate upon it. We may be excited about a passage that speaks to our situation or it is uplifting to us. Far more important than this immediate self-gratification is that God wants us to recognize the true power of His Word, so that we can apply it to our lives daily and share it with others. Pursuing God requires consistent work on the part of the Christian. Think of the newborn baby in his early stages of development. Milk is ideal for those first stages of life, but in order for him to grow healthy, solid foods are introduced to facilitate the development of his body and organs and to further enhance growth. In addition, as he grows, his ability to move, jump, think, and act is also dependent on the types of food he is given. Metaphorically speaking, if we live on milk for our daily meals as a Christian, we will become weak, lethargic, and unhealthy. Our ability to move and be active will be limited, and we will make less of an impact in whatever we do. If we do not absorb God's Word, the meat and daily bread of our salvation, we become weak and useless. Hosea 4:6 explains that God's people are destroyed because they lack knowledge. Studying the book of Hosea will further reveal that the people did not simply lack knowledge because they did not know the laws of God; rather, they actively *chose* to be disobedient and stubborn to the laws of God. In my opinion, to attain this knowledge involves our true love for God, dedication, endurance, perseverance, thirst, vulnerability, faith, trust, and hope in God.

We all have to start somewhere, and accepting Christ as our personal Lord and Savior is the place to begin. After this new birth, we begin our sanctification process by fulfilling God's purpose in our lives when we are in Him. As Christians, we are set apart for God's purposes, but will miss it if we are not pursuing God's will in our lives. Sanctification involves growing consistently toward moral and spiritual maturity because of the Holy Spirit living in us: "And such were some of you: but ye are washed, but ye are sanctified, but ye are justified in the name of the Lord Jesus, and by the Spirit of our God." (1 Corinthians 6:11 KJV)

It is important to emphasize that perfect sanctification is not attainable in this life. In Proverbs 20:9, we read, "Who can say, 'I have made my heart clean. I am pure from my sin'?" Ecclesiastes 7:20 further states, "For there is not a just man upon Earth that doeth good and sinned not." (KJV) In the previous chapter, I mentioned the power of grace. Note that the scriptures evidently emphasize man's inability to be just because of sin; we can certainly agree, then, that grace gives us all the things we do not deserve: life, mercy, compassion, blessings, forgiveness, hope, joy, peace, etc. We fall out of grace when we sin and give in to the temptation of our flesh to neglect the Holy Spirit. As a result, our sin grieves the Holy Spirit, takes us out of fellowship with God, and brings criticism on the Church. Therefore, it is significant to remain faithful and focus on the Word, as our failure to do so not only affects us but also the whole body of Christ. This can deeply affect our process of sanctification.

As I matured in my faith, I began to commit a specific time of my day with the Lord, quiet time when I could sit with Him, talk to Him through prayer, praise Him, and study His Word. I missed those scheduled meetings sometimes, but that did not deter me from continuing to seek God. I craved His Word and asked Him for direction and clarity as I read.

Becoming a member of a Bible-based church played an essential role in my maturity as well. Learning from other mature members in the body of Christ was important in my journey to become closer to God. Previously, I mentioned that I relocated from the States to the Caribbean. Prior to that move, I was a member of a Baptist church in New Jersey. Though my time there was short, I recall many of the services I attended. One thing that stands out to me was the way the members worshiped. They seemed to be engaged in the Spirit, and the presence of that Holy Spirit could be felt in the sanctuary. The melodious chorus of worship songs echoed loudly through the aisles and pews of the church, accompanied by acoustic music, tambourines, piano, and other string instruments, and it was just a phenomenal place to be on any given Sunday. The members worshiped with tears in their eyes, making a joyful noise to the Lord. I sensed it was something bigger and greater than me, and I wanted some of whatever it was. I wanted to experience that outburst of praise, that place of submission.

I also mentioned earlier that I have always been quite a dancer, and back in the days when I visited the clubs, I did not hold back when my favorite songs came on. My love of dancing has never changed, but now I find my rhythm in songs that bring glory to God. Admittedly, I was a little reserved in praising God in public at first, due to my hidden pride. I did not want anyone to see me clapping and praising the Lord, because it just did not look cool. I later came to the harsh realization that I had no problem praising the enemy in public when I used to enjoy the things of the world. I was convicted thereafter about that, and I decided that I would always praise God with all my heart, with the same zeal and passion I had when I was dancing to the rhythm of the world. I would channel that energy and zeal in a new direction as I praised the God of all gods. I wanted to give God my all, so I began dancing to a new tune and for a different reason. I cannot emphasize how much of an impact this has made on me. Unlike the emptiness that lingered long after my nights at the club ended, worshiping God left me with overflowing joy. Inevitably, no matter what I am going through, good or bad, that joy remains. My praise gives me joy, and God gets the glory!

    We worshiped hard, and it was freeing. The teachings from each pastor who stood behind the pulpit resonated with me, and my convictions were as sharp as any sword. There were those days when the truth pierced my heart and I cried out in repentance. Other days, I received a word of encouragement that propelled me to keep the faith and never give in to my circumstances. Sunday after Sunday, I went to church, not because it was routine or because of guilt but because I was hungry. The very pull I had so strongly resisted for years became my driving force. I needed Jesus, and joining the others collectively at church, as the children of God, did something inside of me, something I know I could not have experience individually. Today, that has not changed. I still go to church, and it is not out of obligation. I go because of my deep love for a man who died on the cross for my sins.

When I learned that we were moving, my prayer was for God to direct us to a church community that would foster and develop us as wholesome Christians, one that would teach, inspire, and engage us in a relatable way. I wanted to find a place that would equip us to serve and help to build His kingdom, a church that exercised the philosophy of Bible-based teaching, with love as the common language of its members. I must state here that no church is perfect. Church pews are filled with human beings and are prone to problems because of it. We are all sinners saved by grace, so even in the midst of the body of Christ, there will be challenges, but these should be seen as opportunities for us to grow in faith.

Having prayed fervently for a new church that would meet our spiritual needs and offer us opportunities to grow and serve, when we first moved, we thought we would visit all the Baptist churches on the island and choose the one we felt led to and were the most comfortable with. We drove around for a few weeks and saw many churches of various denominations. Some were Baptist churches, but in the four and a half years since my husband's relocation, we have never made it to any of those. Instead, my husband's co-worker invited us to attend church with her; much to our surprise, it was a nondenominational church. It would be my first visit to such a church, and I was sure it would be my last. Nevertheless, just to be polite, we accepted her invitation and went with her that Sunday.

We were quite skeptical about attending a church we were unfamiliar with. It was a lot for us to absorb that Sunday, and we had mixed feelings. My husband and I had no idea that the church would become our church home for the duration of our assignment there, but to our benefit, we ended up staying and eventually became members and team players. We involved ourselves in ministries and became loyal and committed to the body of our church.

There was definitely a lesson to be learned in this. Initially, I wanted my will to be done, not His. I walked into that church with my own expectations, but those expectations did not necessarily mirror God's standards. I did not allow myself to be open until I prayed and asked God for clarity. Only then did I realize that the Word really was being taught and that the words on the church sign are not nearly as important as the content of the Word that is being delivered. The message clearly declared the truth: that God is the Father and that He sent His only Son to die as a sacrifice for our sins. Eventually, we realized that the message preached Sunday after Sunday was taken directly from the Word of the Lord. Furthermore, the presentation of the Word was convicting in a way that spoke deeply to our hearts. Soon after, we began to experience a real relationship with God, which is far more intimate than just knowing His name. It was a different approach to Christ using the same message about Jesus' love for us and the forgiveness that is available through Him.

Being part of a church family paves the way for a new Christian to grow. We experience countless things, and in church, we encounter people who have once been where we are. Furthermore, being a member of a church community fosters our growth and equips us in our walk with Christ. It is a significant part of maturing and seeking God's righteousness. Similarly, seeking God's righteousness strips us of every mask and reveals in us our sins, and it comforts us with the knowledge that they were appropriated for.

Regular church attendance is a good practice of the faith, but it is much better when your life reflects the teachings you hear there. It is not enough to just go to just warm a pew, for it doesn't end there. In fact, that is only the beginning of a committed life journey. Beyond being in groups and learning the Word, church should present a challenge for you to live out the Word daily. Agreeably, it is easier to read the Word, listen to the Word, and even regurgitate the Word verbatim, but as Christians, our daily test to apply the Word of God poses difficulty, especially when it comes to those issues we do not necessarily agree with.

His Way or Yours

Have you ever chosen only specific scriptures, those that only relate to your situation at the moment or encourage you in a tough time? Do you ever sing praises and hymns without letting the words go beyond the tip of your tongue? If we are being honest, there are times when we leave church with our hearts still heavy and burdened with the cares of this world. Before we even walk out the door, the Word has already left our memory and has become obsolete in our thinking. Do you remember those times when you really tried to internalize the Word or sermon, but it seemed to have little effect on your behavior, if any at all? Let the choir say, "Yes!" I say this not from a place of judgment or condemnation, for I, too, have been a part of the choir.

I believe that the more deeply grounded we are in the Word of God, the more obvious our presence should be. I do not mean to say this in an abrasive way but in a purpose-driven one. I believe our presence should be so bright that everywhere we go, darkness will be exposed by the light in us. This way, people will be convicted to see the truth. Too often, many self-proclaimed Christians live a double-life and compromise our relationship with Christ out of insolence. Can you imagine how this can dissuade people who are seeking the truth, because of the lifestyles we live? Many self-proclaimed Christians live just as the sinners do, without any marked distinctions, yet they expect to impact the world. Though grace abounds, it is not a ticket for us to do whatever we please. In Romans 6:15

(NLT), Paul wrote, "Well then, since God's grace has set us free from the law, does that mean we can go on sinning? Of course not!" When you really study the Bible and Paul's epistles in particular, you will learn that grace is not an excuse for us to no longer uphold the rules that God has for us. Instead, grace helps us to acknowledge our sinful nature and teaches us how to depend on Jesus Christ to transform us daily. As a result of Christ's death and resurrection, we now have access to God. Before Calvary, we were nothing, but because of Jesus Christ, we can now go boldly before God. (Ephesians 3:12) I encourage you to avoid using grace as an excuse to satisfy your fleshly desires. Do not allow sin to be the dominating factor in your life. Instead, allow Jesus to come into your heart and give you true peace.

The scriptures warn us over and over about the poison of sin. Remember that sin comes in all different shapes and sizes, and God does not see one as worse than another. If we break one law and keep the others, we are just as guilty as the person who breaks all the laws. Our lives are really not our own, so choosing to live according to our own standards just does not pass the test. What we do with our lives here will affect our position in the next life. It is important to note that when we live outside of the will of God, we will miss out on promises that are conditional. I am of the belief that David would have answered yes to the former questions. Perhaps that was one of the reasons why he asked the Lord to create within him a clean heart and renew the right spirit within him. (Psalm 51:10) Like David, we must recognize the significance of submitting our entire life to God, for *His* will to be done, not ours.

On a personal level, I thought I had surrendered all to Christ when I got baptized and was serving in the church. As I shared previously, God revealed the areas of my life that I mistakenly thought were under my control. He disciplined me because of His love for me, a love He has despite my bad choices. My mistakes were often time motivated by my pride, and the Bible teaches that pride is sin. Pride says, "I can do it on my own. I have it all under control." Going to church week after week, service after service does not really mean anything if we are not willing to submit our everyday lives to God. This is not easy, but it can be done and has been by many believers, before our time and even presently, all over the world. An enriched Christian life is a process that can only be achieved through Jesus Christ. Sometimes, it may seem as though God wants us to suffer, but even in our suffering, His will is perfect in comparison to the will of the world.

There was a time in my life when I questioned the existence of God. I thought, *If God is so powerful, then why does He allow bad people to get away with evil deeds?*

Every now and then I asked, *Where is He in the midst of all this catastrophic disaster?* In other times, the silence was deafening: *Are you there, God? Do you even hear me?* In my desperation and pain, hearing God can sometimes become difficult, especially when our posture is wrong. God is a loving Father, though, and He does not want His children to suffer. In fact, I believe that during our difficult times, God wants nothing more than for our faith in Him to grow. Psalm 44 teaches that while it sometimes feels as if God is not awake, we should never give up hope. Like God's people then, we must trust in God and wait for Him to help. The kind of sorrow God allows will cause us to be sorry, convict us, and lead us to repentance. At that time, He will extend His arms and receive us.

We live in a world that paints our struggles and trials as taboo; however, as kingdom people, we should not subscribe to that belief. Instead, we must use the opportunity to grow and overcome our struggles victoriously! We can do so with confidence because of the appropriations of our sins. Christ died for us so we can go to Him daily. I call this the ultimate exchange: I received salvation for my sins, and this newfound life has filled me up. God alone can satisfy our deepest longings. Crying out to God and meditating on His goodness gives us eternal peace. What is your posture when we you are going through trials and tribulations? Are you thirsting for a closer relationship with Christ? Are you asking that His will be done? Are you persuaded that He will see you through? We should all examine our hearts, because that is what God sees!

Chapter 6

Faith for the Journey

Perseverance

Pursuing God's righteousness separates us from the standards of the world and redirects us to the power of God's grace. It is in these moments that you realize that had it not been for the grace of God, pursuing His righteousness would be impossible. Paul wrote in Ephesians 2:8 (NLT), "God saved you by His grace when you believed, and you can't take credit for this; it is a gift from God." Notice that the keyword in this verse is "grace." It is important to emphasize that we cannot take credit for where we are in our journey with the Lord. His righteousness does not reflect my own nature, desires, or temperament. Left to me, I would be nothing, but because He chose me and calls me His child, I can humbly seek His righteousness. If I dwell only on what I am capable of, I will never hear the call of the sovereign God on my life. He calls to things far higher than the limits and boundaries we create for ourselves.

Even when we admittedly take wrong turns and mess up our commitments, responsibilities, relationships, health, finances, and other things, we can believe with confidence that pursuing God's righteousness and accepting Christ will inevitably lead us to the throne of grace. This is an ultimate experience that forever changes you, me, and everyone who seeks Him. We are no longer the same, and the power sin has over us slowly dies. We are a new creation, a brand new being. This change is not immediate, but it will happen over a period of time. The amount of that time can only be measured by God and His plans for our lives.

Ever since I was a child, I have heard people say, "Jesus is coming," or, "Jesus is coming soon." When I heard those words growing up, I questioned the legitimacy of this statement. I did not quite understand the subtle yet bold words. As I grew older, I kept looking for Him to come, but that didn't happen. In my young adulthood, I really struggled with it, wondering what was taking Jesus so long, and after a while, I stopped believing altogether and was sure He would never show up. I stopped looking for Christ, but His grace found me! It was not until I confessed my sins and accepted Jesus as my personal Lord and Savior that I truly began to understand the significance of such a statement.

He is surely coming, even if no one knows the time, hour, or day when He will return. For all the years when I was waiting for His return, it was frightening. Back then, I lived my life on the edge and was fearful that if He returned, I would literally find myself in deep Hell. I did not understand that it is not His will that any should perish. Second Peter 3:9 (ESV) teaches, "The Lord is not slow to fulfill His promise as some count slowness, but is patient toward you, not wishing that any should perish, but that all should reach repentance." God loves us more than we can ever love ourselves, and since He wants what is good for us, He patiently waits on us to come around.

    I realized that it would have been a terrible thing for Him to return when I was living in sin, because though God is a God of love, He is also just, and we will all sit before His judgment seat. The scripture has this to say about His justice: "For if we go on sinning deliberately after receiving the knowledge of the truth, there no longer remains a sacrifice for sins, but a fearful expectation of judgment, and a fury of fire that will consume the adversaries." (Hebrews 10: 26-27 ESV) You might wonder what this means. I believe God wants to say to us, "Look, I love you enough to give you free will, to give you choices, but even though you are free to choose, if you live in sin and turn away from me, there will be a consequence." What is that consequence? Romans 6:23 (KJV) answers bluntly, "For the wages of sin is death." However, if we accept Christ and confess our sins, then we will receive eternal life.

I am so thankful today that God, in His unbelievable grace, waited on me and is still waiting to give people a chance to be free, people like me, who have trudged through the depths of sin and have experienced the ugliness of living in darkness. No longer am I a slave to sin. Rather, I am a slave to God's righteousness, as Paul said in his letter to the Romans. (Romans 6:18) It is His righteousness that sets me free.

In previous chapters, I mentioned that our change begins with the renewing of our minds. This later manifests in our actions and our way of living. Nevertheless, we must understand that our salvation is not dependent on anything we do. It is, however, a free gift that certainly strengthens our relationship with God through our faith. It is important to note that our righteousness is not a result of our works but is an end product of our faith in Him by grace. A true relationship with Christ is the ultimate life-changer. When you sin, you will be convicted, and the behaviors and attitudes that hurt God will also be painful for you. You will be poised, thankful, and contented. In summary, you become like Christ. Who is Christ? He is love, so He commands us to love God and to love our neighbors as ourselves. When we pursue God, we pursue love, and we are able to love because of His love in us. His love heals us when we are wounded. It is a love that releases us from hatred, a love that frees us from condemnation and unforgiveness, a love that is wrapped up in a package of grace. Is it attainable? Can we really be like Jesus? Do we really believe in the mighty power of Jesus? We can find solace in 1 Peter 1:3-7, for those of us who feel hopeless: "Blessed be the God and Father of our Lord Jesus Christ! According to His great mercy, He has caused us to be born again to a living hope through the resurrection of Jesus Christ from the dead, to an inheritance that is imperishable, undefiled, and unfading, kept in Heaven for you, who, by God's power, are being guarded through faith for a salvation ready to be revealed in the last time. In this you rejoice, though now for a little while, if necessary, you have been grieved by various trials, so that the tested genuineness of your faith—more precious than gold that perishes though it is tested by fire—may be found to result in praise and glory and honor at the revelation of Jesus Christ." (ESV)

In 1 John 1:9 (KJV), we read, "If we confess our sins, He is faithful and just to forgive us our sins and to cleanse us from all unrighteousness. This one verse provides the only prerequisite to being transformed. It depends only on accepting Christ by the confession of our sins. Accepting Christ is the beginning of a newfound love and appreciation of life. You will begin to live a purposeful life because greater is He that is in you than He that is in the world. (1 John 1:4) You are no longer in subjection to yourself; you now subject yourself to the Holy Spirit and begin to experience the plans of the Lord over your life. This encounter is sure to change you! Does this mean you will never sin again? Certainly not! In Romans 7:15-25, Paul explains this dilemma; he knew what was right, yet his flesh wanted to do what was evil. We are not made perfect in ourselves but in Christ. For this reason, we begin to live life not in our strength but in Christ's.

Imagine a master dancer leading you as his partner. You only have to trust him and move in the direction he is leading and enjoy the choreograph piece. You can have unwavering faith, for God is with us, and in Him, we are secure, no matter what circumstances come our way.

Chapter 7

Living Your Purpose

I was not living a purposeful life before Christ, but thank God I am now able to live for Jesus and be purposeful about it! God knows my every fault and loves me still. I am confident that He is able to do the impossible in me. Are you confident about your belief? Living a purposeful life doesn't mean we will get it right all the time or that things will work out the way we expect them to. Living a purposeful life does mean being committed to Jesus, staying connected to the vine. It means saying, "Not my will, Lord, but let your will be done." It is saying yes when you really want to say no. It is taking on the challenges that seem impossible or taking the paths that don't seem clear. It is staying on the ship, even when it seems the vessel might sink. It is saying wholeheartedly, "I want God's way to be my way."

We learn from scriptures that the fear of a man brings a snare, but whoever leans on, trusts in, and puts his confidence in the Lord is safe and set on high.(Proverbs 29:25) In my studies, I was led to do learn more about the simple word *snare*, so as to fully understand the concept of this scripture. According to The Free Dictionary, a snare can be defined as "something that lures or entangles the unwary." A snare may also refer to "a kind of trap used for capturing animals." Some synonyms include: trap, catch, pitfall, danger, hazard, and peril. I decided to replace "snare" with some of these synonyms and recited, "The fear of man brings a pitfall, catch, hazard, peril, danger…"

Next, I looked up the definition of *unwary*, which that same dictionary defines as "not cautious; not aware of possible dangers or problems." In other words, when we are living a purposeful life, we cannot fall into the peril of following the ways of man, and we must follow the ways of God. However, we can easily fall into danger if we are unaware of them, if we are blinded to the problems associated with following the ways of man and, to a larger extent, the ways of the world. God requires of His children to follow Him and not the standards of the world.

A Christian living a purposeful life is required to leave his or her comfort zone once in a while. Though this can be frightening, God has equipped us with every good thing to do His will. (Hebrews 13:21) It is important to note, though, that even though God equips us, there is still some work on our part. Hence, this is heavily dependent on how obedient we are. You would never to go into combat without your weapons, nor would you go to work without your tools. You would not feel comfortable taking an important exam without studying first. Survival, success, and passing the test depends on proactively arming yourselves with what you have been equipped with.

To know Jesus requires us to put our confidence in Him, and you cannot trust someone you do not know. To know Him involves knowing His Word, the B.I.B.L.E., which can be defined as "Basic instruction before leaving Earth." The Good Book will help you realize that while you may be physically alive, if you are not living in Christ, you are essentially dead. Though you breathe and move, if you are disconnected from the vine, you are nothing. The good news is that salvation is for all of us, and we must only accept it. However, do not be fooled into thinking there is nothing beyond salvation. You can choose to lead a life in which you serve the cravings of the flesh or a life that is driven by God's purpose. How does this look? I'm glad you asked!

You must know, with all confidence, who you are in God and trust Him to lead you as you seek Him continually. Do not fall into the habit of comparing yourself to anyone else traveling the Christian journey. We are all different. Yes, as God's children, we share a collective purpose to lead the lost to the Lord, but the way we do so will be different. God is a God of variety and mystery, and only He knows what our true motives are.

Sometimes, our motives are not of the spirit but of the flesh, and this affects the outcome of what we do. Even then, God has a way of turning things around, and what is meant for our harm can be used for our good and His glory. Never in a million years would I have thought I'd be the witness I am for Christ today. It was not that I did not believe in God, but after making so many mistakes and wrong choices in life, I thought I would be the last one to share the story of God and His infinite mercy. I thank God that the devil is a liar. I have been released and delivered from the shackles of my sins, and today, it gives me great joy and zeal to share the Word of Jesus with others. The truth is that I cannot undo God's love for me, and neither can you. His love is the very reason He sent His only Son, so you and I can be saved. The thought of such love makes me feel a burst of joy in my soul. The psalmist of Psalm 96 (NLT) beautifully articulates this:

"Sing a new song to the Lord!

Let the whole Earth sing to the Lord!

Sing to the Lord: praise His name.

Each day proclaim the good news that He saves.

Publish His glorious deeds among the nations.

Tell everyone about the amazing things He does.

Great is the Lord! He is most worthy of praise!

He is to be feared above all gods.

The gods of other nations are mere idols,

but the Lord made the heavens!"

It is on this premise that I feel so free and so empowered to share the good news of this man who saved me from a broken spirit. He saw my needs and rescued me. When I had no confidence in myself, He renewed my hope. When I was sinking deep in sin, He extended His hand and pulled me out of the deepest, darkest pit. He gave me a new life, a joy that cannot be stolen from me. I did nothing to receive or earn that beautiful gift, so my heart cries out in thanks to God for saving me.

My story may be similar to yours. Perhaps you know of Jesus, or maybe you do not. The truth is that you must know Him for yourself. A relationship with Christ requires a lifetime commitment, for it is a daily journey that can only be completed with Him. We are made to have relationships, and while healthy relationships with other people can be beneficial, it is fundamental that our relationship with men does not skew our faith and hope in the Lord. Though God created us to have relationships with man, it is imperative that we do not fear man to our own demise. We cannot allow the influences, standards, and principles of man to dictate our daily living; we must rely on the infallible Word of God. Consequently, our steps can be thwarted, and we can be misguided or misrepresent what God wants for us. It takes faith for us to depend totally on Jesus. No longer do we view the world with our naked eyes; we look at people and our situations through the eyes of the Holy Spirit. We are now able to see things in the supernatural realm. I understand that it takes time to get to know someone, and even with Christ, that is pretty much what it comes down to. As a Christian, you need to spend time with the Lord, by reading His Word, fellowshipping with other Christians, and serving others and your community.

This relationship cannot be rushed. It must be built over time, and it is built on trust. You begin to understand the nature of God, and you are able to recognize Him in your daily routines and endeavors. I remember that early in my salvation, I was excited and scared at the same time at the thought of following Jesus. Again, I feared I would not be able to endure the Christian life, and I was terrified that I might break the many rules. As time went by, though, I began to grow in my faith, and my anxiety began to fade. Through His Word, I realized the abundance of promises that await me if I stay true to Him. It is not easy, as I have stated many times, but consider how Jesus suffered on the cross for our sins, without ever complaining or quitting. I am encouraged and motivated to trust Him because of His unconditional love, which He proved when He bled for me!

Sculpted

I am a new creation today because of Jesus. Though I am not perfect, my perspective on life has changed because of my experience with the Lord. Today, I am still married to my husband of twelve years, and we have two beautiful children whom we are trying to raise according to the standards and principles of God. We are active members of a beautiful church community where we serve in several ministries and participate in the overall welfare of our church. We are not perfect, for we are still learning about Christ. Of course, none of what we do matters if we are not living a lifestyle that is obedient and pleasing to Christ.

Over the years, I have learned to develop a consistent, persistent prayer life. This is essential because we do not wrestle against flesh and blood, but against principalities, powers, the rulers of the darkness of this age, and spiritual hosts of wickedness in the heavenly places. (Ephesians 6:12) Paul was very clear when he wrote that in our Christian lives, we will encounter spiritual warfare, and we must be prepared at all times to stand our ground against the influence of Satan and our enemies. For that reason, it is imperative that we seek to surround ourselves with others who are persistent in their faith and are truly seeking God. When we serve together in unity, we can rest assured that God is there with us also. It is not time for us to sit back in complacency, to carelessly watch the enemy come into our territory and take what does not belong to him. Instead, it is time for us to stand up and declare that the plans of the enemy be canceled in the name of Jesus! The weapons of our warfare are not carnal, but they are mighty through God, and they can pull down strongholds. (2 Corinthians 10:4) It is important that we be prepared and ready to go at all times, regardless of our present circumstances. The truth is that when we are in God, His Word changes us, and we are not the same. Again, we cannot do it on our own, or we are guaranteed to fail terribly! What are you fighting for? Are you prepared? Are you walking in obedience?

We may encounter much hurt in life, but God will never harm us. Polishing may hurt, and as God peels away the rough layers, we may have to give up some things we used to do or love or places we used to go. Even more importantly, we may be faced with the difficulty of giving up relationships. Are you willing to go the extra mile in spite of the pain? Will your answer be yes, even if it means that you will experience rejection, shame, and loneliness? Oftentimes, we confuse growth with discomfort and problems with challenges. Being a Christian does not exclude us from difficulties or trials; however, our response to our struggles will certainly separate us from the rest of the world. In our weakness, His great strength is revealed. Will it hurt? Yes! There may be days when you feel as though you can't make it, but that is only a reaction in the flesh. Still, during the most painful times in my life, I hear a gentle whisper in the midst of my hurt, and I can feel His peace. Being a student for life—and, better yet, a student of Christ—my confidence in hope truly soars. I wholeheartedly believe that with Jesus in the center of my life, nothing can bring me real harm.

As I neared this point, reaching the final stages of writing this book, I came to realize that this entire process was a healing one for me. It forced me to confront some unresolved personal issues I had suppressed for years, even though I thought I'd already dealt with him. This was a painful revelation for me, and I must admit that after episodes of anger, complaints, and bouts of self-pity, I did not like how I felt and wanted a quick fix. I was hurt and felt discouraged, so I cried out for God to help me. It was in my stillness that God intervened and said, "You asked for my help, and that is what I am doing." I said, "Lord, is there another way to do it?" and He answered, "In order for me to fix you, I first have to break you." Of course I did not like that response, but I knew he was right! God knew I needed to undergo demolition of my old self and reconstruction of my new one. This is the process that is necessary for God to work in us.

My husband's uncle is a bishop, and he once preached a sermon titled "I Am up for Reconstruction." The message resonated with me, and it still speaks to me to this day for a number of reasons. I will not try to retell the sermon in its entirety, as I know I would not do his excellent teaching justice. In a nutshell, though, he compared a person undergoing transformation in Christ to a house undergoing reconstruction. He emphasized that at the site of an old house that is ready for demolition, before reconstruction, many hidden things suddenly show up. Things that were not so transparent before inevitably become visible. Once the walls are torn down and the floors are gutted and removed, everything in the house is exposed. If you have a creative imagination, you can readily identify some of the things that may be present in such circumstances: dust, garbage, materials, roaches, rats, and all sorts of debris. Similarly, when our minds are under transformation, everything that is not of God will begin to surface. This is not to shame us but to show us how deep in sin we really are. This exposure eventually frees us from being addicted to the darkness and allows us to engage us in a new setting, where there is light. Just like that old house being demolished, everything has to be exposed and cleaned up before we can begin reconstruction.

What was most reassuring about the message was that God sees our mess and is fully aware of all our dirt. Nevertheless, it is better for us to be exposed by God than man. When God exposes our true self to us, He will then be able to help us rebuild our souls. Over and over again, we have heard the adage, "God can turn our mess into a message," but beyond the rhetoric of this statement is a significant truth: God has a plan for our lives, and when we are in alignment with His will, there is a guarantee that we will overcome. Now, my conversation has changed from, "Can we do it another way, Lord?" to, "Lord, give me the strength to do your will."I realized I was being polished! Admittedly, this is my least favorite part of my Christian journey, but I cannot emphasized enough how necessary and relevant this process is. Like an old house, in order for rebuilding to take place, demolition has to happen first.

This process takes a lot of work. It is not attractive to see all that inner dirt, but once demolition is complete and the foundation is left standing, then the builder can begin with the upgrade. We can use our imagination to conclude what the final project look like in the end. The Apostle Paul talked about his struggle with the flesh. This struggle was not unique to him; we also encounter daily struggles with the flesh, a perpetual tug-of-war. If not for God's grace, this Christian journey would be impossible. We are saved by grace alone, so we can do His good works. We cannot do things by our own will, and it is important for us to know that we are not alone. God knows our every burden, and He has equipped us to succeed, but we must first be truthful about who we are to Him. Only when we are honest with ourselves and with Him can He begin the good work in us. I had underlying issues of resentment wrapped up in unforgiveness, and God had to indicate to me that I had not truly let go of my hurt feelings, that I had neglected to give that aspect of my pain to Him. In that awakening moment, my heart sank deep into my stomach, and the revelation brought tears to my eyes. I knew then that it was time to live out what God requires of me.

At present, as I continue on this path, my prayer is for all of God's children to rise up to the call and be filled by Him. Personally speaking, I have come a long way, but I still am on that journey. It is important to note that even though our journey may consist of rivers, detours, bridges, roadblocks, delays, and accidents, we can still be at peace through every twist and turn. God has promised that He will be with us, and that should give us enough fuel for our journey. I have found courage in relying on the Word of God. Today, I am empowered by God's Word in my life; though I still struggle with the flesh, my confidence stands in Him. There aren't enough words to express the immaculate power I have found in my relationship with Christ. He has been my comforter, provider, healer, deliverer, Father, Savior, protector, teacher, and leader. He is my rock. I have found the secret of living, and that is having a relationship with my heavenly Father. My days are not long and hopeless, and the fear of dying no longer cripples me. Though my life can be busy and I often feel overwhelmed with responsibilities and obligations, I no longer experience that void in my life. I feel free, confident, brave, and hopeful! I also have a strong passion and desire to just share and spread God's Word all over the universe.

    I am of the belief that if God can change a simple girl like me, then He can do it for you. We can run from our Creator, but we can never hide from His sight or His love. Have you been running? If you choose to run, why not run to Him? The Word teaches that every knee will bow and every tongue confess that Jesus Christ is Lord. (Romans

14:11) Why not confess it now, if you have not done so already?

Many scriptures speak about Christ's second coming, and we must be prepared. I am reminded of the parable of the ten virgins who set out to meet their bridegroom in the night. Five carried their lamps and additional oil, but the other five only brought the lamps, depending on the oil that was in them. It was a long journey, and there were no streetlights in those days. When the bridegroom arrived, five of the virgins went into the wedding banquet, and the door was shut. The other five were left out because they had to go back to get more oil; they were not prepared. To find out what happened to the other virgins, please read Matthew 25, for you will glean much from this story!

We are God's creation, made in His image, and His breath lives in us forever. We can choose to live with Him in eternal peace, or we can choose to live without Him in eternal damnation. Whatever you choose, know today that there is no middle ground. You can stand up for Christ, or you can stand up for anything. The choice is yours!

I have discovered that having a relationship with Christ was the beginning of defining my purpose in this life. I am no longer dependent on man to validate who I am, and I am also encouraged to stand up for who I am and what I believe. I am God's special treasure! Many of God's children do not recognize this or believe it to be true. We suffer from a lack of self-confidence or self-awareness. I am here today to tell you again the simple but solemn truth: We are God's special treasures! I am thankful that I am still being polished by God. There are days when I exercise in good faith, with positive self-esteem and thoughts about who I am, and there are days when I fail to hold on to this truth. Even when I fail, though, I am no longer where I was a few years ago. I realized that the legacy I intend to leave with my children (particularly my daughter in regard to her self-image) must first represent how God sees them. They are fearfully and wonderfully made. I am thrilled to have the opportunity to teach my six- and eight-year-old the true meaning of beauty. I can engage in healthy conversations with my children about how unique they are, just the way God made them. I have also learned how to help my daughter on those days when she compares herself to other girls with different hair texture and skin color. Boys suffer from self-confidence problems as well, so as often as I can, I declare to my children that we are all beautiful people, created for a special purpose.

In addition to teaching them about their self-worth, it is my solemn duty to point my children in the direction of Christ and the beauty He wants to see in their heart. It is phenomenal how children internalize and absorb what is demonstrated daily in their environment. My children are a constant reminder of how great God is, but they also remind me of just how limited my understanding of Him is. I take great joy in teaching my children about the Word of God and introducing them to reading their kids' Bible, and I challenge them to ask questions about their faith. I am very thankful that even though my children are young and inexperienced, they know that there is a God and that He loves them unconditionally. The opportunity to parent my children while we are all being parented by God the Father has taught me much about the grace of parenting and moving in authority under the authority of God. It is during these times that I have to ask God for help and instruction on how to be the best mother I can be.

I believe God gives us children so we can better understand His relationship with us. If we strip away all the wrong things a child can potentially do, at the end of the day, the love for that child remains. Regardless of any difficulties and disappointments we face in raising our children, we still love them indefinitely. Though we are hurt by our children sometimes, that does not change our love. Our love emerges from the day they are conceived in the womb, and as parents, we share a forever bond with our little ones. This bond is irreplaceable, very rare, and different from any bond we share with anyone else. I challenge myself and you that if we love our own children regardless of what they have done, then God, who is eternal and is not man, must love us even beyond the earthly love for our children. The scriptures tell us that there is no greater love than Christ's, who laid down His life for us. God our Father has eternal love for us, and there is nothing we can ever do that will cause His love to fade. This solemn truth gives me hope in seeking God and having a relationship with him, and having this knowledge of God's love has given me peace.

Chapter 8

Knowing Your Worth

An Appeal

God has deposited in my heart through his Son Jesus Christ an overwhelming sense of urgency for His people and for those who are lost. The message, though simple, has existed since the foundation of the Earth, through Jesus' birth, death, and resurrection. That message is that there is hope, for God loves you unconditionally. He is interested in every detail of your life, and He wants a relationship with you!

Do you know Jesus as your personal Lord and Savior? Whatever your response is to that question, Jesus can handle it. He is ready and available to forgive you when you ask for forgiveness. I encourage you not to delay in asking.

The degree of your past sins does not matter, nor does your present situation. Your status and qualifications do not matter. It doesn't matter if you are wealthy or poor, old or young, sinner or saint, sick or well. God has a plan for you because of His Son Jesus. You have a purpose that can only be filled by you, and Jesus cares equally for all people. In order for you to activate that divine purpose you were created for, you must be connected to the vine. If you know in your heart that there is an inner need that is not being met by your daily obligations and routines; if life has become monotonous and deep inside a voice is crying out for help; if your heart aches because something is missing;

if you have been searching tirelessly for the truth and can't seem to find any peace within, then I encourage you today to seek Jesus. Your salvation and faith lies within Him.

I must caution you and emphasize that seeking Jesus will not be an immediate answer to all of your trials and problems. In our microwave and Wi-Fi world, a place where we are all accustomed to instant gratification, it is very easy to slip into that mentality in all aspects of our lives. However, as previously mentioned, to truly know God and to accept and fulfill His will in your life, you must undergo a journey that can only be strongly established over a period of time. Jesus will be the constant change in your life, as only in Him and through Him will you be able to endure this beautiful relationship. You must only start by taking the first step, though, and the rest is like dancing. You can just follow your partner, Jesus, and watch Him lead you in the greatest waltz of your life.

If you lack faith, ask Him to increase it. If you lack hope, ask Him to restore your belief. It is written in the scriptures that Jesus is the way, the truth, and the life. To make a difference in this world is very respectful and admirable thing to do. You may have made indelible impressions and contribution in your field of expertise, and that might be a good thing, but even if everything you do is successful, you will be unable to truly appreciate and understand the extent of your purpose when you are living outside of Jesus. Our good deeds cannot save us, but when we accept Jesus into our hearts, He saves us so we can do good works. "For we are God's handiwork, created in Jesus Christ to do good works." (Ephesians 2:10 NIV) Until we accept Jesus as our personal Lord and Savior, the void will remain empty. I know this from firsthand experience, and that is why I am sharing it with you today.

If you have read through this book, please do not chalk it up to mere coincidence. Much prayer has gone into writing it, and it is also my prayer that you will take this opportunity to repent and ask God to come into your heart and save you. If you have done so already, I pray that something you have read here will strengthen your walk with Christ. The simple plea to invite Christ into your life will require a lifetime commitment. The good news is that you will not be doing it alone. Every step you take, know that God has already gone ahead of you and made provisions for you. There is so much more to your life than what you are experiencing now. If you are already a committed child of God, here is an opportunity to press on through the faith. Know that when God is involved in what we do, there are no limits. It is better to live in the will of God and experience difficulties than to live outside the will of God and encounter riches.

If you are neither here nor there in your belief or you have backslidden and feel unworthy of Jesus' love, I pray you will hold those thoughts captive and subject them to God. Here is an opportunity to share your heart with God. Nothing surprises or intimidates Him. Jesus is waiting on you to be honest about who you are and where you are in your life. We were all born in sin and shaped in iniquity, and God sent His only Son to redeem us from our sinful hearts. If you don't know where to start, pray and ask God to show you; He speaks when we stop to listen. He is the God of yesterday, today, and forever, and He can and should be the God of all of your days, from here to eternity.

Many Bible stories demonstrate God's matchless power and grace. We can link our present generation today to Abraham. Because he believed, he was blessed and counted righteous. God granted him more than he ever could have imagined, and he became the father of many nations. Not only that, but Moses, led by God, had the great privilege of leading the children of Israel out of their bondage with the Pharaoh of Egypt. David, a mere shepherd boy, slew the giant Goliath and was later ordained as Israel's greatest king.

All of those amazing things happened in the Old Testament, but it did not end there. In the New Testament, we find the story of the woman at the well. Anyone who has ever felt like an outsider should read this story often. She was an outcast for many reasons, yet Jesus, a Jew who normally would have had no part in talking to a woman of her ethnicity, took the time to tell her things about herself that no one else knew. He is interested in every detail of our lives! We must also consider the woman who suffered from a blood issue for twelve years; she had such great faith that she was healed simply by touching the hem of His garment. Peter, only a fisherman, became one of the most significant disciples, and he taught the Word and took the expansion of the Church over the byways and faraway, distant places, in spite of great opposition. My personal favorite is Saul, who passionately persecuted Christians for their belief in Jesus but then met Jesus on the road to Damascus. That experience changed him into the man we know as Paul, one of the greatest influencers for Christ and on churches of his time.

There is a myriad of stories, testimonies, and demonstrations of what God has done and what He is able to do, all recorded in the Bible, but once again, there are also more modern examples. Dr. Martin Luther King stood up in faith and fought for equality for all people, despite great opposition and senseless killings in the name of religion, justice, and war. Now, numerous individuals actively demonstrate their faith each day, working and speaking in schools, corporations, governments, churches, and organizations. On a more personal basis, I am here, just a simple country girl with a huge heart to share God, despite my past mistakes and present situations. God has a purpose for each of us, and He has one for you. What is your purpose?

    I will conclude with this, for those of you who might be experiencing a degree of uncertainty or difficulty about Jesus, the Son of God. I understand that it is not easy to believe in something or someone you cannot see, but that does not make it any less real or invalid. The worldview insinuates that there are many gods and that they are all relevant to your faith, because we have the right to choose. If your decision about life is based on the general worldview, that assumption would be correct. However, the only way to really know God is to read your Bible, for this is how He speaks to you and reveals much about Himself and his Son Jesus. That is the God I have spoken so confidently about in the pages of this book: the Godhead, the three-in-one Father, Son, and Holy Spirit.

Have you ever seen the wind? You cannot see it coming or going, but you can surely see it stirring the leaves around or feel it when a draft tickles your skin. At times, it has the intensity to propel things over far distances, to great heights. It may also echo a soft whisper or howl through the treetops. You cannot describe what it looks like, but you know it is there. The Bible teaches us that we cannot understand the marvelous mystery of God with our finite minds. Hence, to be called the children of God, we need faith to believe. Like the wind, I have never seen God, but I have felt Him and have seen the things He has done in my life, in the lives of others, and in our world. I have entered into His presence and experienced His joy. Over a period of time, I have also learned to hear Him speak, and His voice influences the decisions I make about the way I live my life here on Earth. We cannot touch or see the wind, but we know it exists, and we know it has the power to uproot, lash, gust, or pick up anything that gets in its path. So it is with God. We all get to experience the marvelous work of creation, but we often neglect to meet or acknowledge the Creator. The wind is free, as are the beautiful oceans, skylines, forests, and mountains. If the Creator can make these things for our enjoyment at no cost, so can you experience Jesus without any expense to you. He already paid the price when He died on the cross for our sins, so accepting His salvation costs you nothing.

I now close this journey where we first began. Are you connected to the vine? Once you are truly connected, it is inevitable that you will bear fruit. Being watered by Jesus produces good fruit in our lives. An orange tree cannot bear apples, and so it is with every believer in Christ. We must bear fruit that represents the Holy Spirit dwelling in us. It is on that note that the scriptures teach us to "study to shew thyself approved unto God a workman who need not to be ashamed." (2 Timothy 2:15KJV)

Today, wherever you are, ask yourself these questions: "Am I being polished by God, and in the process of my grooming and trimming, am I bearing the fruit of the Spirit? Does my life reflect love, joy, peace, patience, kindness, goodness, faithfulness, gentleness, and self-control?" Whatever your response may be, I encourage you to deal with it now! There is nothing too hard for God. If he can change me, He can change you. Whatever you do, remember that your relationship with Christ is a journey and that change is constant and not a final destination. I pray that you will find Jesus and that His will for your life will be fulfilled, that you will be the polished treasure He has always purposed for you to be!

The End

About the Author

Ylodia M. Robinson

God has purposed us all, in differing ways, according to His will. You know you are living His will when you find yourself living the answers to your prayers. Ylodia Robinson, a prayer warrior, has often prayed a fervent and frequent prayer entreating to live a life in which God's will and purpose are the premise and pillar of her existence.

A lifelong learner as well as a certified educator, Ylodia uses every opportunity for evangelism by sharing God's love. An adept event planner, Ylodia is also the founder of a Praying Wives Club, a member of the Praying Moms Group at her children's school, a mentor for young adults and serves on several ministries at her local church. Ylodia and her husband, Fitz are the proud parents of two wonderful children.

Ylodia is currently working on other projects, and is co-authoring a "Polishing Treasures: Unveiling Your Worth and Purpose, Reflection Journal". For more information:

Go to www.facebook.com/believe.receive.live

www.worthandpurposeblogspot.com

A Testimonial Note

This book has made me feel less alien like; it made me bring up some deep feeling I thought I had buried. To sum them up I would feel like I just didn't deserve to belong to anything . I was not worth the time of day. I would feel alone in a room filled with people or sad when everyone is happy, or drowning in water while walking on land. I know now without a doubt that these things will pass, but only if you ask God to come in and help you, not on your own. I kept failing because I was doing it on my own! I know now that these feelings are just the Devil trying to worm his way into my head and my heart, but with God s' strength and power I can fill these negative feelings with love, laughter, happiness and peace.

I learned that to actually be successful you have to want to let God in, allow His power and strength to calm your busy spirit and evict all negative thoughts from your mind. Not your human power, only with God's strength will you get past the sadness and loneliness. It has brought me some peace within my own head. I feel normal and not like I am a stranger in my own body, if that makes sense. The crazy ocean hurricane that are my thoughts have been calmed to just rolling waves of a quick passing rain cloud. He has forgiven me! "Oh my goodness" He really has forgiven me for all of my sins; and all I need to do is believe that He has forgiven me and then forgive myself. How amazing is that! So simple yet overlooked daily.

Thank you for sharing your life's path, as it made the light bulb in my head go off. I am not alone, and even when I try and I failed, I should just try again! God has not forsaken me and I should not let doubt cloud my judgment because I am God's child. He died for me, for me, thank you Jesus for doing that for me.

Nerissa

www.ingramcontent.com/pod-product-compliance
Lightning Source LLC
Chambersburg PA
CBHW022356040426
42450CB00005B/203